A Soldier's Life

Raintree · OSPREY PUBLISHING

Confederate Infantrymen of the Civil War

Ian Drury · Illustrated by Gerry Embleton

This American edition first published in 2003 by Raintree, a division of Reed Elsevier Inc., Chicago, Illinois, by arrangement with Osprey Publishing Limited, Oxford, England.

For information, address the publisher:
Raintree, 100 N. LaSalle, Suite 1200, Chicago, IL 60602

First published 1993
Under the title *Warrior 6: Confederate Infantryman 1861–1865*
By Osprey Publishing Limited, Elms Court, Chapel Way, Botley, Oxford, OX2 9LP
© 1993 Osprey Publishing Limited
All rights reserved.

ISBN 1-4109-0112-2

03 04 05 06 07   10 9 8 7 6 5 4 3 2 1

Library of Congress Cataloging-in-Publication Data

Drury, Ian.
  [Confederate infantryman, 1861-1865]
  Confederate infantrymen of the Civil War / Ian Drury.
    v. cm. -- (A soldier's life)
Originally published: Confederate infantryman, 1861-1865. Oxford [England] : Osprey, 1993, in series: Warrior.
Contents: Historical background -- Timeline -- Recruitment -- Appearance -- Equipment -- Weapons -- Training -- Tactics _ Skirmishing -- Typical engagements -- Fighting spirit -- Pat Cleburne's career -- Logistics -- Medical services -- Confederate casualties
  ISBN 1-4109-0112-2 (lib. bdg.)
  1. Confederate States of America. Army--History--Juvenile literature.
2. Soldiers--Confederate States of America--History--Juvenile literature. 3. United States--History--Civil War, 1861-1865--Juvenile literature. [1. Confederate States of America. Army--History. 2. Soldiers--Confederate States of America--History. 3. United States--History--Civil War, 1861-1865.] I. Title. II. Series.
  E546.4.D78 2003
  973.7'42--dc21
                          2003005278

Author: Ian Drury
Illustrator: Gerry Embleton
Editor: Lee Johnson
Printed in China through World Print Ltd.

Dedication
To Dee and J.E.B. Drury, our own little Rebel

Acknowledgments
I would like to thank David Isby and Robert Bruce for their invaluable assistance in locating photographs for this book.

Artist's note
Readers may care to note that the original paintings from which the color plates in this book were prepared are available for private sale. All reproduction copyright whatsoever is retained by the Publishers. All enquiries should be addressed to:

  Scorpio Gallery
  PO Box 475
  Hailsham
  East Sussex
  BN27 2SL

CONTENTS

CONFEDERATE INFANTRYMEN OF THE CIVIL WAR

HISTORICAL BACKGROUND

In March 1865 Mary Chesnut was in Chester, South Carolina, where she saw Stephen D. Lee's sadly depleted corps from the Army of Tennessee. The soldiers were returning from the battle of Nashville, the South's bloodiest defeat, heralding the end of the Confederate States of America. Yet the soldiers were singing as they marched.

"There they go," she wrote, "the gay and gallant few, doomed, the last gathering of the flowers of Southern pride ... They continue to prance by, light and jaunty. They march with as airy a tread as if they still believed the World was all on their side, and there were no Yankee bullets for the unwary."

The American Civil War was predominantly an infantryman's war fought by men such as these. Artillery had improved substantially since 1815 and guns could inflict murderous losses if they had a clear field of fire. But most Civil War battlefields were characterized by sprawling forests and broken ground. Cavalry were important for reconnaissance, raiding and rearguard actions but there was little scope for saber charges in the grand old manner when infantrymen armed with muzzle-loading rifles could face such tactics with confidence. Decision on the battlefield rested with the foot soldiers. Ultimately, the Confederacy's survival as a nation would largely depend on the fighting ability of its 642 infantry regiments.[1]

The men who fought in those regiments came from a South badly outnumbered in 1860. The census of that year recorded a population of 5,449,462 whites in the 11 states that fully seceded. Adding pro-Confederate elements in Missouri, Kentucky, Maryland, and Delaware, the number of white Americans from which the army was drawn totaled no more than six million. The northern (white) population was over three times greater.

The Richmond Grays in all their finery, Virginia 1861. Fully equipped with overcoats and backpacks containing spare clothes, many of the volunteer regiments entered the Manassas campaign with wagon-loads of equipment. Many regiments included black servants to wash and clean for enlisted men and officers. (Library of Congress)

All armies are a reflection of the society that creates and maintains them and this was particularly true of the Confederate States, a nation-in-arms. Some 75 percent of the population eligible for military service served in the South's armed forces. For the overwhelming majority this meant joining regiments raised by the individual states. The Confederacy did create a tiny national army in the heady spring days of 1861 – just seven regiments – but it was immediately eclipsed by the state units filled by a rush of volunteers. When the supply of volunteers began to falter within a year, the Confederacy introduced the draft on April 16, 1862. For the first time, American men were subject to

1. LIVERMORE, Thomas L. *Numbers & losses in the Civil War in America* Boston 1902

conscription: a revolutionary step soon followed by the Union.

Having joined his regiment, the experience of the Confederate infantryman would have been familiar in most respects to that of his forefathers during the Revolutionary War. Some Southern soldiers had met veterans of the Continental Army; most had heard the stories of 1777 and of the privations at Valley Forge. Like that previous generation of American soldiers, the Confederates spent most of their time on the march or in camp. Pitched battles were far from everyday events and, while a bloody action might lay many of their comrades low, Southern infantrymen knew they were more likely to die from disease than enemy bullets.

There were important differences from the 18th century or the Napoleonic wars. The firepower of Civil War armies gave the defense an even greater advantage than before. The new weapons and the rough terrain combined to make it almost impossible to destroy an army in a day's battle. Annihilating victory proved an elusive dream for generals on both sides and there were to be no American equivalents of Jena or Waterloo. Battles were every bit as bloody but were seldom as decisive.

The average Confederate infantryman marched to war in 1861 full of confidence. He derided his enemies as city-bred Yankees who would get the whipping they deserved. The Confederate's belief in the inherent superiority of Southern soldiers would endure to the end of the war despite events early in the conflict, such as the bloodbath at Shiloh that cost the South over 11,000 casualties including General Albert S. Johnston.

67-year-old Edmund Ruffin was a bellicose secessionist who claimed to have fired the first shot on Fort Sumter at 4.30 a.m. on April 12, 1861. A member of the Virginia plantation aristocracy, he had campaigned vigorously for an independent Southern nation. Arriving at Morris Island outside Charleston he was made an honorary private in the Palmetto Guard and later fought at Manassas. He could not reconcile himself to the Union victory in 1865 and shot himself on June 18. (US National Archives)

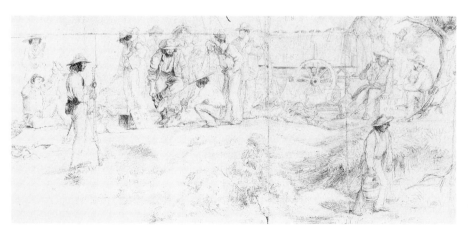

The first sketch received by *Harpers* during the war was this illustration of Confederate soldiers outside Fort Clark, Texas, in March 1861. Fort Clark surrendered to Texas state volunteers on March 19, the day after ageing hero Governor Sam Houston was deposed for not taking the oath of allegiance to the Confederacy. (Library of Congress)

In June 1862 General Robert E. Lee assumed command in Virginia and without delay he began an offensive against the Federal army approaching the Confederate capital. The so-called Seven Days' battles drove back the much larger Union force but at the fearful cost of over 20,000 casualties. Lee then took the war to the North in the vain hope of rallying Maryland, if not Europe, to the Southern cause. Neither hope was realized and the holocaust at Antietam was followed by President Lincoln's Emancipation Proclamation. Northern war aims had gone beyond coercing the South back into the Union; the Confederacy was now fighting for the very survival of Southern society.

In 1863 the twin disasters at Gettysburg and Vicksburg dashed hopes of military victory and European recognition. But the Confederate army fought on. Although the numerical odds were lengthening in 1864, many Confederate veterans proudly re-enlisted at the beginning of the year; united in hardship they remained determined and defiant. By contrast, half the Union soldiers whose terms of enlistment expired in 1864 refused to fight on and left the battle for others to finish.

The fall of Atlanta and Sherman's infamous March to the Sea spelt the end of the Confederacy. And most Confederate infantrymen recognized the bitter truth. Thousands of men deserted, heading back to homes and families. Others remained true to the bitter end – like the soldiers that Mary Chesnut saw in Chester – or Lee's veterans whose surrender at Appomattox was so memorably described by General Chamberlain: "Men whom neither toils and sufferings, nor the fact of death, nor disaster, nor hopelessness could bend from their resolve; standing before us now, thin, worn, and famished, but erect, and with eyes looking level into ours ..."[2]

TIMELINE

1860
November 6 Abraham Lincoln elected President
December 20 South Carolina votes to secede from the Union

1861
January Six more states vote to secede
February 8 The Southern states unite to form the Confederate States of America
February 9 Jefferson Davis elected President of the CSA
March 4 Lincoln sworn in as President of the USA
March 6 Davis calls for 100,000 volunteers
April 12 General P. G. T. Beauregard's guns open fire on Fort Sumter
April 15 Lincoln calls for 75,000 volunteers
May 23 Virginia votes to secede from the Union. North Carolina, Tennessee and Arkansas follow
July 21 First Battle of Manassas

1862
March 23 Battle of Kernstown
April 6–7 Battle of Shiloh
May 25 Battle of Winchester
August 9 Battle of Cedar Mountain

The regulation uniform laid down by the Confederate Congress was never achieved in practice, but this drawing shows a soldier in something approaching it. He wears the frock coat generally abandoned in favor of shell jackets, and his kepi is in pristine condition. Note the small pouch on his belt for percussion caps.
(US National Archives)

2. CHAMBERLAIN, Joshua L. *The Passing of the Armies, An Account of the Final Campaign of the Army of the Potomac. Based on Personal Reminiscences of the Fifth Army Corps* New York 1915

August 29–30 Second Battle of Manassas
September 17 Battle of Sharpsburg (Antietam)
October 8 Battle of Perryville
December 13 Battle of Fredericksburg
December 31–January 2 Battle of Stones River
(Murfreesboro)

1863
May 1–4 Battle of Chancellorsville
July 1–3 Battle of Gettysburg
July 4 Vicksburg surrenders
September 19–20 Battle of Chickamauga
November 24 Battle of Lookout Mountain

1864
May 5–6 Battle of the Wilderness
May 8–12 Battle of Spotsylvania
June 15–April 2 1865 Siege of Richmond and
Petersburg
June 27 Battle of Kenesaw Mountain
November 15 Atlanta burned
November 30 Battle of Franklin
December 15–16 Battle of Nashville
November 15–December 13 Gen. Sherman's
March to the Sea

1865
April 2 Gen. Lee abandons Richmond and
Petersburg
April 3 Richmond burned
April 9 Gen. Lee surrenders to Gen. Grant at
Appomattox court house
April 20 Gen. Johnston surrenders to Gen.
Sherman ending the war

Charleston Zouaves parade for the camera at Castle Pinkney,
South Carolina, in 1861. They wore a grey uniform with a red
kepi, collar, and epaulets. The officers appear to be wearing
the dark blue frock coat specified by South Carolina
regulations of 1861. Note the drummer and fifer on the far left
of the photograph. (Library of Congress)

RECRUITMENT

Most Confederate infantrymen were in their early twenties. Over 90 percent of them came from rural communities of fewer than 2,000 people, reflecting the low level of urbanization in the Confederacy. It is hardly surprising, then, that 60 percent of Confederate infantrymen were farm workers; over 20 percent were laborers and only about one in ten came from a profession or a white-collar job. However, while most Southern soldiers came from the country, the same was true of their opponents: only 25 percent of the Northern population lived in settlements of more than 2,000 people and the teeming slums of New York provided a disproportionately low number of recruits. It was a countryman's war.

The most important difference between the ordinary soldiers of the Civil War and their predecessors is that we can read about their experiences in their own words. In 1860 the USA as a whole had the third highest literacy rate in the world – only Sweden and Denmark surpassed it. Some 80 percent of the white population of the South was literate, a higher proportion than Great Britain (at 67 percent) but lower than the Northern states (at 90 percent). Many ordinary soldiers wrote home, describing their experiences in every detail. There was no real censorship and they were free to tell their folks anything they liked. If they were so demoralized they contemplated desertion, they said so. If they thought their officers were incompetent fools likely to get them killed, they had no hesitation in venting their feelings. But most letter writers were primarily concerned with news of their families and homes.

One of the strangest ironies of the Civil War is that most of the soldiers fighting to preserve slavery had nothing to do with the South's "peculiar institution." From a white population of over eight

million there were just 380,000 slave-holders: on average less than 25 percent of Southern families owned slaves or were involved with them in some capacity, for example overseeing on the plantations. The exact proportion varied, with those from the Deep South more likely to be connected to slavery – in Mississippi and South Carolina about half of all white families owned slaves.

Confederate soldiers who did have a connection with slavery were most likely to come from a family that owned just a handful of slaves – half of all slave-holders owned five slaves or less. Only about one in eight slave-holders possessed more than 20. This figure became a key threshold when the Confederate Congress exempted from conscription one man in every family owning 20 or more slaves. The theory was to avoid denuding the big plantations of the white manpower necessary to maintain order. In practice the "Twenty Negro Law" caused considerable resentment, giving the unavoidable impression that poor men were having to fight while rich men stayed at home. Congress later imposed a $500 charge for this exemption but only after the damage had already been done.

Conscription itself was a dramatic step. When the war began men enlisted for 12 months. As a result the army was in danger of falling apart by the beginning of 1862. The Conscription Act gave the government control of 18 to 35-year-olds for the duration of the war. While such centralization gave the South a huge advantage, exemptions, as we have seen, and constitutional opposition undermined its effectiveness.

The Confederacy was outmatched by the North in many respects, but it did have one advantage: trained officers. Of the eight military colleges in the USA in 1860, seven were in the South. The Virginia Military Institute provided a third of the officers of Virginia regiments in 1861 alone: and of the 1,902 men who had attended the V.M.I. no less than 1,781 took up arms for the Confederacy.

Above: Two men from the 25th Virginia cavalry equipped with pistol and bowie knife. Confederate infantrymen also tended to sport extravagant knives, particularly at the beginning of the war when they carried a great deal of excess baggage and many still lacked modern firearms. (Library of Congress)

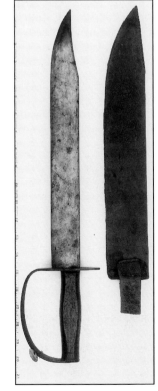

Right: A good example of a locally manufactured fighting knife. Today they adorn the walls of several museums. They may look ferocious but few soldiers would get to kill an enemy soldier with cold steel. (Virginia Historical Society)

APPEARANCE

The Confederate Congress established uniform regulations for the army in 1861. The infantry were to wear a sky blue kepi with a dark blue band, a "Cadet Gray" double-breasted frock coat with sky blue facings, and sky blue trousers.

At the outbreak of the Civil War regiments dressed in the Zouave style appeared in both armies. The two most famous Confederate units were predictably recruited in New Orleans: the Louisiana Tigers and the 1st Louisiana Zouaves, also known as the "Pelicans." Although purporting to show the Tigers at New Orleans in 1861, these men are probably from the Louisiana Zouaves since their trousers are of a solid color (red) as opposed to the white/grey bed ticking worn by most of the Tigers. The jackets were dark blue, the sashes pale blue, and the fez red. (Library of Congress)

No record survives, however, of any such uniform ever being issued.

In practice, the Confederate infantryman wore whatever he found most comfortable. Indeed, during several phases of the war, he wore whatever he could lay his hands on. An English visitor to the Confederate army in 1861 recorded the "uncouth and even sorry appearance" of the infantry. The soldiers wore slouch hats – even straw hats – and wore just shirts and trousers; but "besides his musket and cartridge box, every man had a canteen, most men a blanket and haversack. A more suitable equipment for summer service in Virginia could hardly have been devised."[3]

Slouch hats were much preferred to the regulation French-style "little caps." In winter rain or summer sun, a wide-brimmed hat was simply more practical and it usually doubled as a pillow. Shapes varied from low-topped bowler-shaped hats to high-crowned "beegums" but medium-brimmed slouch hats were the most favored. The more raffish infantryman might pin the brim up on one side and possibly add a feather to complete his dashing appearance.

The regulation frock coats were usually replaced by short-waisted single-breasted shell jackets. "Gray Jackets" became a synonym for "Johnny Reb" early in the war. As for the color, "Cadet Gray" proved difficult to achieve once the blockade cut off supplies of imported dye. The Southern equivalent was made from copperas (sulphate of iron) and walnut hulls, resulting in a distinctly yellowish brown shade of grey. A Union soldier who was captured at Antietam observed that only a single Confederate regiment wore regulation Confederate grey uniforms, describing the rest of his captors as being clothed in "homespun butternut."

"Butternut" they may have been, but they were certainly not "homespun." Many surviving Confederate uniforms were factory-made; their varying grey/brown hues are the result of cotton cloth vegetable-dyed to a shade of grey. Modern experiments at the University of North Carolina have shown that after only a few weeks' exposure to sunlight, such a uniform will begin to turn brown. The factory-made cloth was cut by tailors hired by the Confederate government and then hand-sewn by female piece workers. Variations abounded between the different factories; surviving jackets have four to 12 buttons (sometimes captured US brass ones) and include almost any combination of shoulder straps, chest padding, pockets, belt loops and decorative piping.

Underneath his jacket, the infantryman wore a shirt and/or vest. The latter were not issue items

3. Blackwoods Magazine 1861, quoted in COMMAGER, Henry S. *The Blue & the Gray* Indianapolis 1950

but were often made with a military-style cut, buttoned to the throat and with a collar.

The sky blue trousers, as prescribed by the new regulations of October 8, 1862, seem to have been a rarity too. Contemporary descriptions of Confederate trousers usually describe them as grey and most examples in museums today are various shades of butternut. Confederates who actually wore sky blue pants had probably taken them from a Yankee. Trousers were usually worn tucked into the stockings – more practical when moving through vegetation and a way of keeping wood ticks and other "critters" from climbing up the trouser leg. Underneath their trousers most soldiers wore cotton underwear – common issue items – which were trouser-shaped with a button fly and ties at the back to secure them.

Coats were a problem for the Confederate soldier who had to carry every item of his equipment, whatever the season. However desirable a thick coat was when the snow was on the ground, few men wanted to carry one in typical summer temperatures of 90°F and with 90 percent humidity! "The men came to the conclusion that the trouble of carrying them on hot days outweighed the comfort of having them when the cold days arrived," remembered Carlton McCarthy a Southern soldier. Most infantrymen discarded their coats in the spring and "trusted to capturing one about the time it would be needed."

The Union army was regarded as a useful source of most items of kit. Overcoats and trousers plus cartridge boxes, ammunition, and rifles could all be pressed into service immediately. Despite the obvious danger, many Confederates even took to wearing captured blue jackets. On April 24, 1862, The Richmond *Daily Despatch* claimed that three-fifths of the Confederate army at Corinth were wearing Yankee hats and coats after overrunning the Union camps on the first day of Shiloh. Confederate commanders issued frequent orders for such captured jackets to be dyed grey, threatening to confiscate any that were not.

In any era, the infantryman's greatest concern is his feet. Without proper footwear even a short march can turn into an agonizing struggle of endurance. Straggling was an endemic problem in Confederate armies and the frequent lack of boots

Company K, 4th Georgia Regiment "The Sumter Life Guards," April 1861. Only on garrison duties (and then only in the early part of the war) did Confederate regiments present so uniform an appearance. Note the frock coats worn by the NCOs. (Library of Congress)

was a major cause of it. The battle of Gettysburg was precipitated by Pettigrew's brigade marching to the town because it was reported to have a large stock of shoes. Perhaps as many as one in four infantrymen returning from the subsequent battle had to march without boots, making their way south along the grassy banks beside the stone-filled roads. Many divisions organized the shoeless men into separate commands for the march, proceeding by shorter stages. At least they were marching home in summer. The Army of Tennessee left a trail of bloody footprints in the snow as it retreated south after the battle of Nashville: perhaps the most enduring image of that long-suffering army.

EQUIPMENT

In 1861 the newly assembled Confederate regiments marched to the front carrying a vast assortment of baggage. They carried full sets of cutlery and changes of clothes ready to make a splash in Washington when they planted the Stars and Bars on the White House lawn. Many officers and some soldiers brought along black servants to attend to their needs. None of this lasted long once on campaign: the servants were soon sent home, although a few were retained as cooks. All excess gear was discarded without much ceremony. General Richard Ewell expressed the prevailing Confederate view during the Valley Campaign: "The road to glory cannot be followed with much baggage."

Some soldiers carried their kit in large knapsacks but most preferred to roll their gear in a blanket and wrap it in a captured Union oilcloth. They then tied the ends of the resulting tube together. The wheel-shaped blanket roll was then slipped over the left shoulder and right hip. Most men also wore a little haversack slung over the right shoulder so that it rested on their left hip. This was used to store tobacco, a pipe, a small piece of soap, apples, corn, and any other useful items the soldier managed to acquire on the march.

Tin canteens were supposed to be issued but a high proportion of men had wooden ones constructed like miniature barrels two or three inches high and about eight inches across. US metal canteens were also a common sight. "Stonewall" Jackson's men and other hardened campaigners even discarded their canteens as surplus weight. They just carried a tin cup ready to drink from any stream they happened on during the march or in action.

Only two items were essential to the lightly equipped Confederate infantry: cartridges and caps. The soldiers were issued with a rectangular leather cartridge box that held 40 rifle cartridges, and a little square pouch for the percussion caps. Both were supposed to be attached to the infantryman's belt but soldiers carried them any way they pleased. The cartridge box was not popular and many soldiers threw theirs away, carrying the ammunition and percussion caps in their pockets instead, or even carrying separate powder and ball.

South Carolina State Troops at Charleston, August 1861. This city, more than any other in the South, impressed European observers with its passionate hatred of Yankees. The Confederates dug extensive earthwork fortifications around the city, packing them with a formidable array of heavy artillery that would defeat the US Navy's attempt to break into the bay in 1863. The trench warfare that followed on Morris Island rivaled anything seen at Petersburg later in the war. (Library of Congress)

WEAPONS

There was to be one significant change in the equipment of the Confederate infantry from 1861 to 1865. At the beginning of the war a large part of the army was armed with smoothbore muskets, mostly percussion-fired, though flintlocks were issued when there was nothing else. As the war continued, the majority of the infantry obtained muzzle-loading rifles. In the early war years it was not unusual for a regiment, or even a company, to be equipped with several different types of weapon.

In 1860 less than 25 percent of Federal weapons were stored in the South. The following year the Confederate Ordnance Department, headed by Major Josiah Gorgas, inherited 8,990 .54 caliber rifles, 1,765 .58 caliber rifles and 972 .69 caliber rifled muskets from United States arsenals now inside the Confederacy; including the various states' arsenals, the South had fewer than 20,000 modern rifled firearms at the beginning of the war. That the newly raised infantry regiments had any weapons at all was due to the help of the US War Department under John B. Floyd. In the last year of the Buchanan administration, Floyd supplied Southern governors with 105,000 smoothbore muskets and 10,000 .54 caliber rifles. Small wonder that he did not stay at Fort Donelson to be captured wearing a Confederate uniform in 1862.

At the beginning of the war 80 percent of the American arms industry was based in the Connecticut valley. Although the Confederate government soon had rifles in production at Richmond using machinery and parts captured at Harper's Ferry the supply of Southern-made guns never met the demand. Confederate infantrymen were often armed with .58 caliber Springfield rifles captured from the enemy, or with imported foreign weapons. The latter ranged from the excellent British Enfield .577 rifled musket to poor-quality smoothbore muskets from Austria, Belgium, and southern Germany.

Confederate infantry in the eastern theater, particularly those in the Army of Northern Virginia, were generally better armed than their comrades in the west or the far south. The regiments that fought at Manassas were at least armed with military weapons even if some were obsolete. By contrast, almost half the soldiers then assembling under General Price in Missouri were armed with whatever

Born just outside New Orleans, Pierre Gustave Toutant Beauregard was the real architect of the near-triumph at Shiloh, and he resumed command after A.S. Johnston's death. But he fell into disfavor with President Davis and spent the mid-war period in South Carolina. In 1864 he defended Petersburg against Butler's large army, saving the Confederate capital from being overrun while Lee was locked in battle with the Army of the Potomac. (US National Archives)

they could bring from home. Several thousand had no firearms at all, many others carried shotguns or hunting rifles, mainly squirrel guns. The latter certainly came in useful given the shortage of rations but their value in combat was questionable.

General Lee's vigorous attacks on the Army of the Potomac in the Seven Days' battles not only drove back McClellan's mighty host, they also resulted in the capture of 30,000 Springfield rifles. The acquisition of these modern weapons and the loss of 20,000 men in the process left the Army of Northern Virginia armed almost exclusively with muzzle-loading rifles. The battles of Second Manassas, Harper's Ferry, and Fredericksburg provided a further 40,000 rifles. A few men carried smoothbores into 1863, but after Chancellorsville in May, Lee's men were just as well armed as their opponents.

Company B, 9th Mississippi regiment, photographed by J.D. Edwards at Warrington Navy Yard, Pensacola, in 1861. The soldier on the far left has been identified as James Pequio, the one in the checkered trousers stirring the frying pan is Kinlock Falconer and the man with the shovel is John Fennel. (Library of Congress)

When General A.S. Johnston took over the Western Department in 1861 he soon found himself having to order fresh supplies of flints for the obsolete flintlocks carried by many of his infantry. At the battle of Mill Springs, Kentucky, in January 1862 heavy rain made those carried by many Confederates unusable. The best-equipped regiment defending Fort Henry had Tower Pattern muskets once carried by the militia during the war of 1812. However, it should be emphasized that their Union opponents were in a similar position. At Shiloh, Sherman's division required six different types of ammunition for its motley array of weapons. Many of Grant's army carried percussion-fired .69 caliber muskets converted to rifles; others were issued with Belgian or Austrian weapons of equally dubious accuracy.

The Kentucky and Tennessee campaigns of August–December 1862 netted the Confederates in the west another 27,000 rifles bringing the total number of weapons captured to over 100,000 for the year. Complaints about lack of weapons do not arise again until late 1864 when heavy losses and the collapse of the Southern railroad net led to renewed shortages.

The Confederate infantryman's appearance was a far cry from the martial splendor of the militia in pre-war Charleston or New Orleans. It was rough and ready, simple and practical. One man watching Lee's army cross the Potomac in 1862 described them as "the dirtiest, lousiest, filthiest, piratical-looking cut-throat men I ever saw. A most ragged, lean and hungry set of wolves. Yet there was a dash about them that the Northern men lacked …"[4] – a description few Confederate infantrymen would have quarreled with.

Manufacture and maintenance
In 1861 the Confederacy had only two rifle works, small arsenals at Richmond and Fayetteville, North Carolina. More ominously, almost all gunpowder came from the North. Unless the South could develop its own manufacturing facilities quickly, the Confederate armies would have no ammunition. Fortunately, Josiah Gorgas, the new chief of ordnance appointed in April 1861, proved to be an administrative genius. No Confederate army was ever defeated for lack of weapons or ammunition.

4. Century Magazine Vol. 70 No.2 1906, quoted in MURFIN, James V *The Gleam of Bayonets* 1965

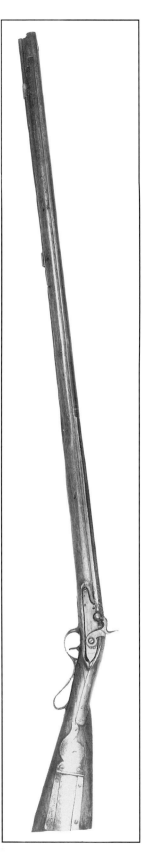

Left: The Confederacy pressed every available firearm into service. This rifle is stamped "Virginia Manufactory, Richmond 1806" on the lockplate and was converted to percussion during the Civil War. The ornamental iron patch box is in the form of a snake and bears the legend "Don't tread on me." The stock is walnut with iron furniture. Only 200-240 of these .45 caliber rifles were ever made but most were converted to percussion and surviving flintlocks are worth a small fortune today. (Virginia Historical Society)

Below: Company A, 5th Regiment of Georgia Volunteer Infantry. "The Clinch Rifles" of Augusta, GA, photographed on May 10, 1861. Note the combination of civilian shirts, pre-war tall kepis and wide-brimmed slouch hats. (Virginia Historical Society)

Under Gorgas' direction, the Confederate government expanded its existing facilities and established new large arsenals at Augusta and Macon in Georgia; Charleston and Columbia in South Carolina; and at Selma in Alabama. A key section of the Ordnance department was the Niter and Mining Bureau. Headed by the equally capable Isaac M. St John, it had to find sources of niter, metals, coal, and other chemicals needed for weapons manufacture. It undertook geological surveys, bought mineral rights and hired mining companies.

By the end of 1862 the eight Confederate arsenals were manufacturing 170,000 cartridges per day plus another 1,000 rounds of field artillery ammunition. Lead production had reached 155,000 pounds per month.[5] Enterprising Ordnance officers appealed to Southern patriots for any metal that could be scrapped. Church and plantation bells were melted down for bronze cannon barrels and – in the spirit of true sacrifice – copper alcohol stills were melted down to make percussion caps for rifles.

5. OSTERHOUDT, Major Henry T. *Towards Organized Disorder: The evolution of American infantry assault tactics 1778-1919* Unclassified DTIC technical report, Alexandria 1979

Although some 20 different types of rifle were manufactured for the Confederate forces [see accompanying table], the majority of Confederate infantrymen were armed with captured or imported weapons. All were relatively easy to maintain and had few working parts to go wrong. This was just as well because only the Springfield rifle and Enfield rifle made by the London Armory had interchangeable parts, while on earlier weapons or other imported firearms all parts were individually made and it was no more than a happy accident if the lock from one musket fitted another. Thus it was not always possible to cannibalize broken weapons to make others serviceable. Some features of British firearms were not universally popular: an Englishman serving in a Confederate regiment was astonished to see his comrades removing the elevating rear sights of their new Enfield rifles. They said they were accustomed to judging their aim "by eye"!

The Confederate soldier certainly seems to have looked after his gun; many contemporary descriptions, particularly by English observers, contrast the sorry state of the soldier's clothing to his well-presented rifle. A clean rifle was far more accurate than one that had fired a couple of dozen rounds and a regiment's first volley could be decisive. Black powder fouls rifle barrels very quickly, making it difficult to ram down fresh cartridges. If the soldier failed to get the charge and ball right down to the breech before firing, the rifle was likely to misfire or bulge its barrel. Excessive

fouling also increases the recoil so the butt starts to bruise the firer's shoulder however well he is holding it. Depending on the conditions and the quality of the cartridges, a soldier could expect to fire about 30 shots before the barrel needed cleaning. If he had to carry on regardless then it was pot luck if he hit anything.

After battle many soldiers found their rifles needed more than a thorough cleaning before they were serviceable again. Gettysburg revealed how human error compounded the inherent problems of black-powder rifles. Some 37,000 rifles were left on the battlefield; 24,000 of them were loaded – 18,000 of them with more than one round, the rest incorrectly. Common mistakes included loading the whole cartridge without opening it or putting the bullet in first and ramming the powder down on top of it. Some of the multiple-loaded rifles had six or more cartridges hammered down the barrel. In the stress of combat some infantrymen had clearly been going through the motions, oblivious to the fact that they were not firing. It is unlikely that every rifle accidentally rendered unserviceable was left on the field. A few soldiers in every company probably found themselves with an accidentally blocked barrel when they came to clean their guns. If it is assumed that for every unserviceable rifle left at Gettysburg there was a similarly useless weapon in the hands of an infantryman, over 30 percent of the infantry had effectively disarmed themselves during the course of three days' fighting!

At the beginning of the war Confederate infantrymen armed with their own hunting rifles often carried loose powder and shot, loading as required. As military weapons were issued, they were supplied with paper cartridges containing the bullet and powder. These were made by hand, rolling the paper around a specially shaped wooden cylinder. The open paper cylinders were placed in a

Manufactured in Columbus, Georgia, c.1862–64, these .58 caliber muzzle-loading weapons were made in three versions: the musketoon or artillery carbine with a 24 in. barrel; a cavalry carbine with 23 in. barrel and large sling swivel; and a 33 in. barrel rifle. The locks were of the US Model 1841 type. This is the rifle and it carries the adaptor for a saber-type bayonet. (Virginia Historical Society)

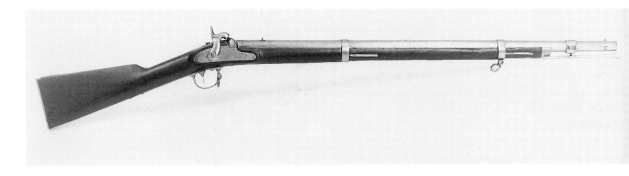

RIFLE MANUFACTURE IN THE CONFEDERACY[6]

Name	Place of manufacture	Caliber	Production*	Notes
Asheville Armory	Asheville, NC	.58	c.300	Crude copies of the Enfield Short Pattern rifle.
M.A. Baker	Fayetteville, NC	.52	?	Percussion conversion of the US M1817 rifle.
J.B. Barrett	Danville, VA	.54	900	Hall Model 1819 breech-loading rifles and carbines converted to muzzle-loaders.
Bilharz & Hall	Pittsylvania, CH, VA	.58	400–700	22" barrel carbine based on Springfield Model 1855, once attributed to Hodgkins & Sons of Macon, GA.
Chapman	Tennessee?	.54	<100	Copies of the US M1841 rifle.
Cook	New Orleans, LA	.58	2,000+	Copies of the Enfield rifle built by two British brothers first at New Orleans, then at Athens GA.
Davis & Bozeman	Central, AL	.58	750+	Copies of US M1841 rifle.
Dickson & Nelson	Dawson, GA	.58	?	Muzzle-loaders with lockplates styled after the US M1841. Most of the few surviving examples dated 1865.
Fayetteville Armory	Fayetteville, NC	.58	2,000+	Copies of the US M1861 rifle, some from captured parts from Harper's Ferry.
Lamb & Co.	Jamestown, NC	.58	?	Based on US M1841 rifle; the state of North Carolina ordered 10,000 but only a few hundred were ever delivered.
Keen & Walker	Danville, VA	.54	280	Breech-loading carbine similar to the US Maynard carbine with a breech block like that of a Perry carbine. All made May–September 1862.
Mendenhall, Jones & Gardner	Greensboro, NC	.58	?	Based on US M1841 rifle. Few made.
Morse carbine	Greenville, NC	.50	1,000	Morse breech-loader built from machinery captured at Harper's Ferry, mainly for South Carolina state troops.
Morse musket	Greenville, NC	.71	Very few	Percussion-fired smoothbore muzzle-loader.
J.P. Murray	Columbus, GA	.58	c.500	Rifles and carbines using the lockplate of US M1841 rifle.
Richmond Armory	Richmond, VA	.58	?	Based on the US M1861 rifle and built in larger quantities than any other Confederate rifle. Machinery captured at Harper's Ferry.
Sharps carbine	Richmond, VA	.52	5,000	Copies of the M1859 Hartford-made Sharps.
Tallahassee	Tallahassee, AL	.58	500	Copies of the Enfield rifle built at the Confederate Armory at Tallahassee c.1864.
Tapley carbine	Greensboro, NC	.52	?	Breech-loader invented by Jere H. Tapley during the war. Patented in 1863 but only a few hundred made.
Todd	Montgomery, AL	.58	Few	Copy of US M1861 rifle.
Tyler	Tyler, TX	.54	?	Assembled from Austrian and Enfield parts and built in .57 caliber as well. Several hundred made.

tray and charged with powder from a lever-operated dispenser. The elongated bullets fired by Civil War rifles were pressed rather than cast and they were added to the cartridge base first. Some European manufacturers were still making them with the nose of the bullet facing the powder, so the soldier had to reverse it. after pouring the powder down the barrel.

6. FLAYDERMAN, *Norm Flayderman's Guide to Antique American Firearms* 4th Edition, Northbrook, Illinois 1987

TRAINING

To the Confederate infantry training meant drill; hours and hours of marching and maneuvering in different formations until the actions became instinctive. Recruits had to learn to act in concert, the ultimate aim being to deploy in line of battle in the right place at the right time, an ability critical to success on the battlefield. Since the men were already accustomed to the use of firearms there was little attempt at weapons training other than learning the manual of arms. The ability to shoot straight was taken for granted.

For the new recruit – or for the officer of volunteers who had been a planter only a few months earlier – military drill seemed a mysterious business. The volunteers of 1861 learned by weeks and months of painstaking effort, impressing European observers with their precision. The credit for this goes to harsh task masters like "Stonewall" Jackson, who had his men at Harper's Ferry drilling for seven hours every day.

American infantrymen had been drilled in European-style linear formations since the Revolutionary War. The Mexican War had demonstrated the US Army's mastery of such tactics and many of the men appointed to senior rank in 1861 had been junior officers under Scott or Taylor. Under their leadership, the armies of the Civil War were drilled according to the same basic manual *Rifle and Light Infantry Tactics*. Written in 1855 it was closely based on the French regulations of 1831 and 1845. The author was Lieutenant-Colonel William J. Hardee, who had graduated from West Point in 1838 and visited several European armies in 1840. From 1856 to 1861 Hardee was Commandant of the US Military Academy when he resigned to join the Confederacy. A revised edition of his work entitled *Rifle and Infantry Tactics* had just been published.

In 1861 the terms tactics and drill were all but synonymous. Hardee's manual was almost exclusively concerned with drill: step-by-step instruction in the words of command and necessary evolutions to change from one formation to another. Beginning at company level and working up to the deployment of a whole corps, it explained all the maneuvers developed for European infantry in the wake of the Napoleonic wars. The infantry were to fight in a two-deep line and there was no

Robert B. Hurt, Jr., Adjutant of the 55th Tennessee Infantry, has armed himself to the teeth with a Mississippi Rifle, fighting knife, and revolver. (Eleanor S. Brockenbrough Library, The Museum of the Confederacy, Richmond, Virginia)

longer any distinction between "line" and "light" infantry. Battalions had no discrete skirmishing unit as all soldiers were supposed to be able to fight in open order if required. Skirmishers were to fight in four-man groups on a frontage of 20 paces, the groups 20–40 paces apart. Half of a company ordered to skirmish would remain in close order, acting in support of the men in the frontline.

Hardee's manual explained many ways by which soldiers could deploy from close to open order. It detailed every possible method by which an infantry battalion could form a column by companies, divisions, platoons or even files. How to advance or retreat through a defile was thoroughly covered and the importance of one formation was heavily stressed: the square for defense against cavalry. Because of the complexity of the maneuver and the urgency with which it usually needed to be formed, the manual insisted that infantry regiments must frequently practice forming squares.

Union soldiers used the same manual. Major-General Silas Casey's *Infantry Tactics* published in 1862 made its author a good deal of money but it differed only in a slight rearrangement of paragraphs.[7] He too emphasized the importance of forming square to defeat an enemy cavalry charge.

Hardee's manual ran to over 500 pages, Casey added a third volume to make over 700. Neither has a single word to say on fighting in woods, entrenching or advancing by rushes, which were all features of Civil War battles as early as 1862. They merely describe the basic mechanics of infantry maneuver in the age of smoothbore percussion muskets. As always battlefield experience led to change. It was a gradual process and an uneven one. The first Union infantry attack on Bloody Lane at Antietam was made in a shoulder-to-shoulder line that would not have been out of place in the 18th century. The Army of Tennessee's attack at Franklin two years later was equally anachronistic. In both cases the attacking regiments suffered horrendous casualties. At other times and on different battlefields, soldiers would evolve their own methods, fighting in loose waves of skirmishers.

Despite the evolution of battlefield tactics recruits entering the Confederate ranks in 1864 were drilled in the same way as their predecessors in the heady days of 1861. The extent to which later recruits were taught the new realities of battle tactics depended on their regimental officers and where they were stationed. In the Armies of Tennessee or Northern Virginia they could benefit from the experience of veteran officers and NCOs, but if they were posted in the deep South they might be led by men who had seen little action since the war began.

In his memoirs General Sherman observed how "few battles in which I participated were fought as described in European text books, viz, in great masses, in perfect order, maneuvering by corps, divisions and brigades. We were generally in wooded country and though our lines were deployed according to tactics the men were generally found in strong skirmish lines taking advantage of the ground ..."

7. OSTERHOUDT, Major Henry T *Towards Organized Disorder: The evolution of American infantry assault tactics 1778-1919* Unclassified DTIC technical report, Alexandria 1979

General Benjamin Franklin Cheatham was one of the Army of Tennessee's most stalwart officers, even if he was probably drunk during the battle of Murfreesboro. His Corps fought very hard at Atlanta in July 1864 and it led the advance into Tennessee at the beginning of Hood's ill-fated campaign. (US National Archives)

TACTICS

In March 1861 the Confederate Congress decreed that infantry companies would consist of 64–100 privates. The maximum was raised to 125 in October 1862 but this was seldom achieved in practice. Companies were formed in two ranks, 13 inches apart with each file occupying a 24-inch front. A company was commanded by a captain who positioned himself on the far right of the formation with his first sergeant behind him. The captain was supposed to have three lieutenants, four sergeants, and four corporals at his command too, although once on campaign he would often have fewer junior officers and NCOs at his disposal. It is worth noting that Confederate infantry companies had fewer officers and NCOs than their Union counterparts: US regulations called for a captain, two lieutenants and 12 NCOs to run a smaller company (64–82 men and usually at the low end of the scale). Since casualties amongst officers were often very high, many battles would end with the senior surviving captain commanding the regiment, and the command of an infantry company could often fall to a second lieutenant or even a sergeant.

According to the practice of the pre-war army the company was equally sub-divided into two platoons. The second lieutenant marched behind the right platoon and the third lieutenant behind the left. The corporals were all posted in the front rank on the right of each platoon.

Regiments fought in a single line of companies with the regimental colors in the center. The colors were guarded by half a dozen men, and soldiers on both sides would take suicidal risks to protect their own or seize those of the enemy. Regiments were officially commanded by a colonel with a lieutenant-colonel, a major, an adjutant and a sergeant-major under him. If all were present for duty, the colonel would ride behind the center with the adjutant behind the company on the right flank and the sergeant-major behind the company on the far left. The major would be stationed between the colonel and the sergeant-major; the lieutenant-colonel between the colonel and the adjutant.

With the regiment in line, two experienced sergeants would be positioned as guides, one on either flank. Selected for their accurate marching, they helped keep the regiment on course when the whole line advanced. With all of a regiment's ten companies deployed side by side, the line could be 250 yards long: a formation that was difficult enough to maintain when advancing over open country. When confronted by fields of crops, fences, ditches, and woods the formation was easily disrupted. And a disrupted formation was unable to obey commands promptly – so it could not react quickly and fire control was impossible. Hence the officers' insistence on repetitious drill when the regiment was in camp.

Confederate infantry were taught to march into battle in column and deploy into line to fight. Firing could be by volleys fired by the whole regiment, by each company in turn or by platoons or even by files. Firing by files was the favored method in Hardee's and Casey's manuals and firmly endorsed by "Stonewall" Jackson. He thought it gave the enemy the impression he was facing a larger force than if the regiment fired by company or regimental volleys. However, the fire-eating Jackson went on to say:

"But my opinion is that there ought not to be much firing at all. My idea is that the best method of firing is to reserve your fire till the enemy get – or you get to them – to close quarters. Then deliver one deadly, deliberate volley and charge!"[8] This is

8. HENDERSON, Lt Col G. R. F. *Stonewall Jackson* London, New York and Bombay 1903 Vol 1

A fine view, sadly cracked on the original plate, of Wigfall's Mess, 1st Texas Infantry, 1861. This sort of log cabin was the last word in comfort for the soldiers in winter quarters. Subsequent winter camps would not be so permanent. (Eleanor S. Brockenbrough Library, The Museum of the Confederacy, Richmond, Virginia)

how Jackson's men fought at Bull Run and it was exactly in accordance with pre-war tactical doctrine. At West Point, Denis Hart Mahan had taught a generation of cadets that musket volleys delivered by the regiment in line of battle were to be followed by a bayonet charge.

Unfortunately these "volley and charge" tactics belonged to another era. Like the company and regimental evolutions described by Hardee's and Casey's manuals, they had been perfected in the days of smoothbore muskets that had an effective range of about 60 yards. The flintlock weapons of the Revolutionary and Napoleonic wars frequently misfired and were highly inaccurate. The muzzle-loading rifles of the Civil War were far more reliable since they were percussion-fired, and they had an effective range of 250 yards. Three rounds per minute was considered a practical rate of fire so a regiment of 600–700 soldiers would send about 2,000 rounds down range every minute.

To advance into that across an open field of fire was to invite disaster. Cobb's brigade, defending Marye's Heights at Fredericksburg, shot down wave after wave of Union infantrymen as they came on in steady lines from a ravine some 300 yards from the Confederate position. Officers inspecting the field the following day found a few bodies 50–100 yards from the firing line, but the main mass of bodies lay over 100 yards away. Each attack had melted away outside the effective range of smoothbore muskets in an irrefutable demonstration of the power of the rifle.

Skirmishing

The longer range of the soldiers' rifles made battlefield maneuvering very difficult. Once under rifle fire, regiments making an attack tended to advance in successive lines of skirmishers, anticipating the Prussian tactics of 1870. The neat lines of the drill books did not last long once the bullets were flying. One Confederate officer observed, "Whoever saw a Confederate line advancing that was not as crooked as a ram's horn? Each ragged rebel yelling on his own hook, and aligning on himself!"[9] It was customary to deploy two of a regiment's ten companies as skirmishers, covering the front and flank of the main line.

The artist William Ludwell Sheppard served in the Confederate army. His paintings and sketches record the everyday life of the Southern soldiers as much as the great battles. Here a Confederate skirmish line advances. (Eleanor S. Brockenbrough Library, The Museum of the Confederacy, Richmond, Virginia)

Higher proportions could be used; sometimes a brigade might send one of its regiments ahead almost entirely in open order. The exact proportion of skirmishers would vary with the nature of the ground and the tactical circumstances.

Union general Lew Wallace likened skirmishers to the antennae of insects, probing around the main body to give warning of the enemy. Failure to deploy skirmishers could be disastrous. There are numerous instances of regiments marching forward in close order only to find the enemy much closer than expected. At Antietam the 4th and 8th Pennsylvania Reserves drove scattered groups of Confederates out of the East Woods and pursued them into the cornfield beyond. They were about 30 feet from the rail fence when the 2nd and 11th Mississippi and 6th North Carolina regiments rose up from behind it and delivered a crushing volley. The Pennsylvania Reserves broke and fled, carrying away another regiment behind them.

How far the skirmishers should be from the main line depended on the terrain and the tactical situation. If the skirmish line was established a considerable distance away from the main body, a

9. HENDERSON, Lt Col G.R.F. *The Science of War* London, New York and Bombay 1905

further company or two might be ordered forward in support. Hardee's manual suggested a skirmishing company would deploy one platoon (half its men) in open order with the other platoon in close order 150 paces to the rear. The supports were to fill vacant places in the line, pass forward ammunition and serve as a rallying point should the enemy force the skirmishers back. If another company was sent in support of the skirmishing company (or companies), Hardee suggests it should be posted 400 paces behind the supports.

To deploy forward into open order an infantry company was first ordered to halt. The second platoon stepped three paces to the rear and the first platoon split into groups of four soldiers. The leftmost of these groups marched directly ahead while the others moved off in succession, marching diagonally. Once they were about 20 paces from the group to their left they marched straight forward. When all the groups of four were marching forward at 20-pace intervals, the captain ordered them to halt and the individual soldiers spread out until they were all about 5 paces apart. The section commanders stationed themselves about 30 paces in the rear, each with four men taken from the reserve. If a bugler was available, they would have one to pass on signals from the captain.

While the first platoon opened out, the second platoon marched to its right until it formed up 150 paces behind the skirmish line. It was commanded by the first lieutenant. The captain stationed himself about 70 paces in front with a bugler and

four men – so he was half-way between the skirmishers and their supports.

The mechanics of forming a skirmish line may sound overly formal but the writers of the manuals were aware of how easily tactical control could be lost. They admitted that the intervals between each sub-unit were for guidance only and that the nature of the ground would dictate what actually happened. If the entire company was thrown out in open order it followed the same procedure as for the first platoon's deployment above.

Advance by rushes

Advancing by rushes was another tactical method that appeared early in the war. Described by some contemporaries as "Zouave tactics" or the "Indian rush" this was another departure from the close-order linear tactics used in the Mexican War. Confederate soldiers developed a habit for advancing by rushes "because it was the only way to work sensibly" as one of them put it. Their opponents were equally quick off the mark (at least in the west). Sigel's men at Pea Ridge and the regiments that attacked Fort Donelson all advanced by rushes rather than attacking in close order.

However, it was only when attacking under fire that looser formations were adopted. When fighting on the defensive, regiments needed to mass their firepower and generally deployed in accordance with the manuals. Indeed, regiments occasionally doubled on each other – the infantry defending Marye's Heights lined the wall four men deep. Several officers marveled that no Confederate was accidentally shot by his comrades. In the Wilderness some Confederate infantry adopted a different means of doubling their firepower: using more than one rifle. Brigadier-General Evander M. Law described how Confederate soldiers went in front of

The 9th Mississippi Regiment in camp, 1861. Few Confederate soldiers would see such tented encampments again: on most campaigns the men would have to sleep out under their blankets only. (Eleanor S. Brockenbrough Library, The Museum of the Confederacy, Richmond, Virginia)

their breastworks where they gathered up the rifles and cartridge boxes of the dead and wounded. "If they did not have repeating rifles they had a very good substitute."[10]

Entrenchments

The American Civil War was by no means the first conflict to involve the extensive use of entrenchments. The armies of Caesar and Pompey routinely fortified their positions during their war for control of the Roman Republic. However, with the long-range firepower of rifled muskets and overhead cover to protect themselves against artillery, entrenched Civil War infantry could be very difficult to shift. In the Army of Northern Virginia Confederate infantry discovered this the hard way during Lee's sustained offensive against McClellan in the Seven Days' battles. The most notorious incident occurred at Malvern Hill when assaulting Confederate infantry suffered severe losses attacking a well-fortified position packed with artillery. Ironically it was the Confederates who began the practice – Magruder's men had delayed the Union advance up the Peninsula by occupying a formidable line of entrenchments.[11]

Confederate infantrymen did not call them trenches. They described them as "ditches" and dug more and more of them as the war continued. In the west, the Vicksburg campaign was concluded by a 47-day period of trench warfare. The long series of rearguard actions under Joe Johnston a year later were dominated by fortified lines. The lines got longer and longer as superior Union forces worked around the flanks and eventually the Army of Tennessee had to pull back to a new position and repeat the process. When Sherman lost patience and attacked at Kennesaw Mountain the result was Malvern Hill in reverse: 3,000 casualties and no breakthrough.

At Vicksburg and in the Army of Northern Virginia's debilitating six months around Petersburg the soldiers lived under fire all the time. Bombardments by field artillery, siege guns and mortars took place by day and night. Depending on the season it was either too cold and wet or too hot and humid to sleep in the "ditches," and the Union gunners took full advantage.

Thomas P. Gooch, Company C, 20th Mississippi Infantry, was one of many Confederate soldiers, particularly in the western theater, who had to face rifle-armed Yankees with only an ancient flintlock. (Eleanor S. Brockenbrough Library, The Museum of the Confederacy, Richmond, Virginia)

Tactics vs artillery

The rifle-armed infantry of the Civil War had a great advantage over the infantry of the Napoleonic period. Their weapons were able to match the effective range of the field artillery's deadliest weapon, canister. Furthermore, since they fought in much more open formation, infantry were less vulnerable to artillery despite the increased range and power of mid-19th-century field guns. Pre-war artillery tactics stressed the offensive use of artillery as in Mexico but many attempts to push the guns forward ended in failure during the Civil War. If the infantry could establish a firing line within a few hundred yards of a battery, they were often able to drive the guns off or at least to force the gunners to cease fire and lie down. Union casualty returns suggest that field batteries rarely suffered heavy losses, tending to pull back and save their guns. Sometimes they left it too late, the horse-teams were shot down and their cannons became prized trophies.

10. LAW, Brig-Gen Evander M. "From the Wilderness to Cold Harbor" *Battles & Leaders of the Civil War* New York 1888

11. DOWDEY, Clifford *The Seven Days: The Emergence of Lee* Wilmington 1988

Suppressing enemy artillery by steady rifle fire demanded that the troops be in good order and not in a hurry. But Confederate infantry were often on the offensive, attacking Federal positions supported by artillery. A frontal assault on a battery could be a very hazardous business. At Antietam the 1st Texas infantry lost 174 men out of 226 present for duty. This is widely regarded as the highest percentage loss of any Confederate infantry regiment in the war, and it resulted from an advance that turned into a firefight with a battery of 12-pounder Napoleons at less than 50 yards range, rifles against double charges of canister. The regiment was also subjected to close-range musketry from as many as three Union regiments once its attack stalled, but it was the artillery that checked the Confederate attack. As for the gunners, Campbell's battery (Battery B, 4th US Artillery) were also engaged by other elements of Hood's division and lost 40 men. Four of their six guns had no one left to man them.[12]

During the Confederate infantry attack that won the battle of New Market, the 700-strong 51st

12. PRIEST, John M. Antietam: *The soldiers' battle* White Mane Publishing, Shippensburg PA 1989

Right: The M1841 Percussion Rifle, also known as the "Mississippi Rifle," was made for the US Army at Harper's Ferry c.1846–55. It was also manufactured by several States for their own militias. South Carolina ordered 1,000 of these rifles from Palmetto Armory, Colombia, South Carolina, in the early 1850s. The lockplate is marked with a palmetto tree just forward of the hammer. (Virginia Historical Society)

Below: Charleston Cadet Zouaves guard Union prisoners-of-war at Castle Pinkney, Charleston, in August 1861. Most of the PoWs were captured at Manassas and would later be exchanged. (Library of Congress)

Confederate fortifications at Manassas, photographed in March 1862. It is a common misconception that the Civil War saw a steady progression toward "trench warfare." Some commanders and some armies relied on earthworks from early in the war while others disdained to take cover throughout the conflict. (US National Archives)

Virginia advanced on the extreme left of Breckinridge's line. To the regiment's front, uphill and resting their flank on the Shenandoah river were two six-gun batteries of 12-pounder Napoleons. The Federal cannons opened fire with canister, driving the 51st VA to ground and inflicting about 100 casualties. The attack stalled. But the Confederates gained the upper hand in the ensuing firefight that developed along the line. The 51st VA took part in the general advance that followed the defeat of a Union cavalry attack and the Federal batteries ordered up their limbers. One battery escaped but the infantrymen concentrated their fire on the other. They shot 17 horses including five from a single horse-team, forcing the Federals to abandon three of their cannons.

Hardee's and Casey's manuals do not at any point explain how an infantry regiment was to fight enemy artillery. Casey's longer work includes a system for deploying a corps of all arms; the artillery were to be distributed in support of the firing line. The actual tactics employed by Confederate infantrymen against Federal guns had to be worked out on the battlefield.

Tactics vs Cavalry

The terrible threat from cavalry that the manuals warned against failed to materialize. Ignoring their drill books, infantry on both sides received cavalry attacks in line and stopped them with firepower alone. There were only a few recorded instances of infantry forming square. At the battle of Olustee, Florida, in 1864 the inexperienced Colonel of the 64th Georgia ordered his equally green regiment into square, believing he faced a cavalry attack. Fortunately Brigadier-General Colquitt managed to get the regiment back into line before the Union artillery batteries could concentrate their fire.

Confederate infantry seldom faced large formations of cavalry prepared to charge in the Napoleonic manner. Most Union mounted charges were made by isolated regiments, often to try to win time for artillery batteries to withdraw. The 5th US Regular cavalry tried this at Gaines Mill, 300 sabers attacking the victorious brigades of Longstreet's Corps. The Confederate infantrymen simply halted and opened fire, emptying 50 saddles and hitting six out of seven officers.

A similar number of Federal cavalry followed Brigadier-General Elon Farnsworth in his charge at Gettysburg. Overrunning Confederate skirmishers behind Devil's Den, the 1st Vermont cavalry rode around in a complete circle as Confederate regiments turned to shoot at them. They suffered 65 casualties before retiring; Farnsworth's horse made it back to the Union lines but Farnsworth himself lay dead with five bullets in him.

At the battle of New Market, Breckinridge's infantry division was attacked by eight regiments of Federal cavalry (about 2,000 sabers) but the Confederates made no adjustment to their formation. The infantry and supporting artillery opened fire as the horsemen emerged from the wooded ridge. The cavalry broke, suffering about 100 casualties. Their low percentage losses may indicate a lack of enthusiasm noted in several other units of Sigel's command, or the equal lack of confidence in Sigel's abysmal leadership.

The battlefield tactics of the Confederate infantry diverged from the pre-war manuals from the very beginning of the war. As the war progressed they became quite distinct from parade ground evolutions. Against cavalry attacks the infantry no longer bunched themselves in square, creating a dream target for enemy artillery in the process. If cavalry charged, the infantry simply shot them down. It is tempting to speculate what might have happened if Union horsemen had behaved like those of France or Germany in 1870, but the fact remains that they did not. Federal cavalry only became an enemy to be feared when they began to fight dismounted with breech-loading carbines. Against Union infantry and artillery, Confederate foot soldiers evolved new, looser formations that took advantage of the ground and reduced their casualties. As Lt.Col. Henderson observed, the infantry tactics of the Civil War represented a dramatic break with the past. In later campaigns in Europe and Asia other armies would learn the same lessons, but often only at equally horrific cost.

TYPICAL ENGAGEMENTS

For the ordinary infantryman battle was a unique experience for which few were prepared. Their commanders might have seen combat in Mexico but most Confederate private soldiers were less than ten years old when Lee, Jackson, Bragg, Davis, Johnston, and the others were winning their spurs. Aside from the 1850s invasions of Cuba launched from New Orleans, military experience was very limited in the pre-war South. While the Confederate forces included nearly 300 ex-US Army officers, only a few dozen enlisted men from the US regular army are recorded as joining the rebels. Although there was a vicious guerrilla war already under way in Kansas, nothing in the young lives of the Confederate volunteers could prepare them for the chaos and horror of a Civil War battlefield. Few nations have ever gone to war with such bellicose enthusiasm as the Confederate States, but Southern patriotism was to be sorely tested in the battles that followed.

In most major battles between 1861 and 1863 the Confederates took the tactical offensive. Southern armies adopted a defensive posture at Antietam, Fredericksburg and Vicksburg while their initial attack at Shiloh was followed by a defensive battle the next day. However, the other eight largest engagements were all Southern attacks: Seven Pines, the Seven Days', second Manassas, Perryville, Murfreesboro, Chancellorsville, Gettysburg, and Chickamauga. More often than not, Confederate infantrymen found themselves attacking superior numbers of Union soldiers, backed by larger numbers of cannons.

Even after 1863 several senior Confederate commanders had not abandoned the offensive. The great defensive battles in Virginia during the spring and summer of 1864 came about because Grant was able to launch his attack first. Lee had fully intended to launch an offensive of his own but was unable to land his blow first because the Confederate logistic system had all but disintegrated. In the western theater by contrast,

Confederate prisoners under guard in a Union camp in the Shenandoah valley, May 1862. The bell tents occupied by the Federals were seldom seen by the Confederate soldiers, who usually slept under nothing more than a blanket. (US National Archives)

John B. Hood led the Army of Tennessee out of its entrenched positions and began a series of offensive battles that would not end until he was overwhelmingly defeated at Nashville.

The psychology of the Confederate infantryman is dealt with in more detail below, but it is worth noting here that remarkably few Confederate soldiers had reservations about the assault tactics favored by some of their commanders.[13] One dissenting voice was General Daniel Harvey Hill whose observations, published in *Battles & Leaders*, have been widely quoted: "We were lavish of blood in those days, and it was thought to be a great thing to charge a battery of artillery or an earthwork lined with infantry … The attacks on Beaver Dam Creek, on the heights of Malvern Hill, at Gettysburg etc., were all grand, but of exactly the kind of grandeur which the South could not afford." Significantly, most comments about the folly of attacking earthworks were to be penned by Union soldiers.

The Confederate soldier became a master at entrenching. In both east and west the Confederate forces were short of trained engineer officers but infantry regiments proved adept at selecting their own defensive lines. Union officers were astonished at the rapidity with which Confederate soldiers could fortify their positions, not to mention the tenacity with which they then went on to defend them. One of Meade's staff recalled that Confederate infantry could dig themselves rifle pits in a day; if left undisturbed for a second day, these would be linked into a regular parapet with artillery batteries in line. A third day would see an abatis of felled timber and brushwood placed in front of the trenches (performing the same job as barbed wire would do in 1914–18) and some overhead cover added to the line. "Sometimes," he lamented, "they put this three days' work into the first twenty-four hours."

The transition of Confederate infantry tactics from offensive operations to the defense of trench lines was not a straightforward progression. Beauregard had strengthened part of the Confederate line at Bull Run, even though some soldiers had complained at "doing the work of Negroes" and some fieldworks had had to be completed by slave gangs hired from nearby

Lt-Gen Thomas "Stonewall" Jackson is one of the few men who really have become legends in their own lifetime. From the moment he took over his first command, Jackson drilled his men with remorseless energy, and it paid handsome dividends. He was a passionate believer in offensive tactics, favoring a "volley and charge" rather than a protracted firefight. Jackson also proved an outstanding strategist and his campaign in the Shenandoah valley would be taught in military academies for a century after his death. (US National Archives)

plantations. Several senior Confederate officers remained firmly wedded to maneuver in the open and were reluctant to entrench. "Stonewall" Jackson, supported by J.E.B. Stuart, urged Lee to assault the Union bridgehead at Fredericksburg rather than remain on the defensive. Lee himself did not order his army to dig in at Fredericksburg until the night after the great Federal assault. Lee did not entrench his position at Antietam even when fully aware that McClellan's greatly superior army was poised to attack. The result was the bloodiest single day in American military history. Lee did order trenches to be dug at Chancellorsville, although some of the work was countermanded by Jackson, and even on the first day of the Wilderness battle in 1864 Lee did not dig in. Only the relentless pressure of Grant's much

---

13. With the possible exception of Hood, the morale of the Army of Tennessee plunged after Franklin and the first day of Nashville. Bragg was another unpopular commander, but most criticism relates to his tough disciplinary measures, especially the shooting of deserters.

larger army compelled the Army of Northern Virginia to fight from trenches.

General John B. Hood launched a headlong attack whenever he had the chance and blamed the soldiers of the Army of Tennessee for the failure at Jonesboro. "It seems the troops have been so long confined to trenches, and had been taught that intrenchments cannot be taken," he wrote, "that they attacked without spirit and retired without proper effort." Those same soldiers would make a superhuman effort a few months later at Franklin, sacrificing 5,500 men and losing five of their generals assaulting the Union earthworks.

The "Hornet's Nest"

The struggle for the "Hornet's Nest" at Shiloh is typical of the bitter fighting encountered by the infantryman in many Civil War engagements. The "Hornet's Nest" ranks with Antietam's "Bloody Lane" or the "Bloody Angle" at Spotsylvania Court House, although it was not even a particularly strong position. A half-mile stretch of abandoned road, it formed a slight depression but was not a sunken road like "Bloody Lane"; it was on rising ground that overlooked the Confederates and it was the only place in the center where the Confederates had a covered approach to the Union line. There was open ground to either side, swept by Federal artillery. The "Hornet's Nest" exercised a magnetic attraction for the Confederates: over a five-hour period no less than ten, and possibly as many as 12, separate infantry assaults took place against this position. By the end of that sanguinary Sunday afternoon some 18,000 Confederate infantry had attacked the position which was defended by 4,300 Union troops at the most.[14] However, the Confederates never succeeded in making a coordinated effort: the largest single attack involved only 3,700 men. The Confederate assaults were carried out with great bravery and at tremendous cost: but these piecemeal frontal attacks simply piled up more bodies in front of the Union line.

After witnessing several abortive bayonet charges, Gibson's brigade was ordered forward to take its turn. The 1st Arkansas and the 4th, 13th and 19th Louisiana regiments charged and were driven back; they rallied and charged again. Although the brigade commander and all four regimental colonels pleaded for artillery support or for a flank attack, they were ordered to go in with the bayonet a third and fourth time by General Braxton Bragg. The brigade was shattered and Bragg eventually ordered up another brigade, which had been repulsed from the same position some hours previously but had now reorganized and replenished its ammunition. Braxton Bragg was a harsh disciplinarian and president of the Confederate army Temperance Society. His insistence on such crude tactics certainly contributed to the Confederate failure at Shiloh, and Bragg's subsequent career would be marred by more serious errors of judgement.

14 McDONOUGH, James L. *Shiloh – In Hell before night* The University of Tennessee Press 1977

Some of the dead from Jackson's Corps at Antietam. Of the 3,400 men present for duty, 226 were killed in action and nearly 1,100 wounded: a casualty rate of 61 percent. The Confederate infantrymen fought their first great defensive battle under Lee without entrenching their position and, although outnumbered by 2 to 1, they defeated the succession of Federal attacks. Total losses were about 12,500 for the Union and 13,700 for the Confederacy: it remains the bloodiest single day in American military history. (Library of Congress)

The "Hornet's Nest" eventually fell after Brigadier-General Daniel Ruggles organized a massed battery of some 62 guns. It took him about an hour to assemble and the steadily increasing volume of artillery fire pinned down the Union riflemen while Confederate infantry worked their way around the flanks. Their position turned, the remaining 2,000 or so defenders of the "Hornet's Nest" finally surrendered: their determined stand had deprived the Confederates of victory. Grant's army had been driven back but not right into the river – and Buell's army had arrived, giving the Union forces a 3 to 2 numerical advantage for the following day.

In contrast to the sluggish approach march of the Confederate army at Shiloh, the speed of "Stonewall" Jackson's men earned them the nickname the "foot cavalry" a few months later in Virginia. A series of lightning maneuvers left their Federal opponents bewildered and beaten.

The tireless Jackson was certainly a dedicated trainer and in his case, success bred success. His soldiers were spurred on by their victories. However, Jackson's uninspired performance during the Seven Days' proved that even the most iron-willed commander could not stave off the effects of chronic fatigue indefinitely. The Seven Days' battles were hardly a triumph of organization for either side, Robert E. Lee's aggressive tactics often proving beyond the capacity of his army. But he learned, and he selected the senior officers who were to command the major formations of the Army of Northern Virginia for the rest of the war.

Although there were some embarrassing exceptions, the Confederate infantryman was generally blessed with better commanders than his

The cornfield at Antietam where several US regiments were shot down at close range as they blundered into the Confederate line. They had no skirmishers in front of them to provide any warning. Federal General Lew Wallace likened skirmishers to the antennae of insects, feeling ahead of the main body. The corn stands as high as a man, providing excellent concealment if no cover from bullets. (Author's collection)

The Burnside Bridge at Antietam seen from the Confederate end. This was defended by a thin screen of Confederate infantry occupying rifle pits on the steep bank overlooking the river. In a tragi-comic assault, the Union regiments suffered heavy losses trying to rush the bridge – when the shallow water could have been waded without difficulty. Burnside's fumbling advance was held up for several vital hours, allowing Lee to concentrate on his left and center. (Author's collection)

Union counterpart in the early years of the war. The natural confidence of Confederate soldiers seemed to be entirely justified in 1862 after McClellan was driven away from Richmond and Pope was humiliated at second Manassas. If the Sharpsburg campaign was a disappointment, the defensive triumph at Fredericksburg and the incredible victory at Chancellorsville certainly led the Army of Northern Virginia to enter the Gettysburg campaign with justifiable optimism.

Unfortunately for the Confederacy, the western armies did not share the good fortune of the Army of Northern Virginia. Confederate leadership in the west was divided and uncertain, and it faced a more competent enemy. Pemberton failed at Vicksburg and Braxton Bragg proved sadly out of his depth commanding the Army of Tennessee. The soldiers suffered the vagaries of the high command with great stoicism: Bragg and Hood became the subjects of various songs as they lost their men's confidence. Stanley Horn recorded a ditty composed in the wake of Franklin and Nashville. To the tune of *The Yellow Rose of Texas*, some of his men were singing:

"So now I'm marching southward;
My heart is full of woe.
I'm going back to Georgia
To see my Uncle Joe.
You may talk about your Beauregard
And sing of General Lee,
But the gallant Hood of Texas
Played Hell in Tennessee."

FIGHTING SPIRIT

The majority of Confederate infantrymen were in their early teens during the bitter political battles of the 1850s. How far they were affected by local, let alone national, politics it is difficult to judge. While local politicians condemned the Northern abolitionists in blood-curdling language and the newspaper editors preached secession, the future Confederate infantryman was more likely to be found at home behind a plow, helping his father and elder brothers on the family farm. However, the approach of the 1860 presidential election probably did increase the political awareness of the young men who would soon volunteer for military service as their states left the Union.

A famous study of a Confederate infantryman with his full equipment: Private Thomas Taylor, Company K, 8th Louisiana Infantry. (Eleanor S Brockenbrough Library, The Museum of the Confederacy, Richmond, Virginia)

President Jefferson Davis emphasized that the South was fighting for the "sacred right of self-government." His first message to the Confederate Congress after the surrender of Fort Sumter stated that the South sought "no conquest, no aggrandizement, no concession of any kind ... all we ask is to be let alone." That last phrase was certainly the key to the motivation of the Confederate soldiers: they took up arms to defend their homes and their way of life against the Yankee army of invasion then being assembled by Abraham Lincoln. It was not the constitutional issues that mattered to the Confederate volunteers, but it was the imminent threat of invasion by a Northern army. One Confederate, captured by Union troops in June 1861, was asked why he was fighting – "because you're down here," he answered.

Thus the Confederate infantryman did not regard himself as fighting for "the peculiar institution" even after President Lincoln expanded Northern war aims from the restoration of the Union to the abolition of slavery and a consequent social and political revolution. However, while only a minority of Confederate soldiers owned slaves, they were violently opposed to emancipation. The Yankee desire to free the slaves was regarded as the first step in creating a society in which blacks were equal in all respects to white men – a concept which, it should be stressed, was completely unthinkable in most parts of the North as well as the South in the 1860s.

The Confederate soldiers regarded themselves as morally and socially superior to their opponents, who they would often describe in their letters as the "scum of the earth." The Union army was seen as a motley collection of slum dwellers from the Northern cities and low-class immigrants from Germany. They were thieves and tricksters intent on despoiling the South; they sought to ravage Southern women but shrank from Southern manhood. The letters of Confederate soldiers are peppered with references to Union cowardice while even grudging mentions of enemy bravery are few and far between.

Combat experience modified the Confederates' views, since whenever the armies were in close contact there was usually some fraternization. Informal truces were arranged not just to bring in the wounded, but to pick blackberries, fill canteens or listen to each other's musicians. Union and Confederate soldiers often exchanged tobacco for coffee or other items in short supply. Even shovels were sometimes borrowed from the enemy not just for burial parties, but to dig entrenchments!

While many frontline soldiers were prepared to suspend hostilities at least on a temporary basis, some Confederates were ready to stop altogether by 1864. There were two main reasons: an increasingly bleak military outlook tended to breed defeatism, and among the poorer soldiers there was a growing feeling that they were risking

Alfred R. Ward's sketch of Confederate prisoners being marched to Frederick, Maryland, in August 1863. Like most Confederate infantrymen, they wear broad-brimmed hats in a variety of styles rather than the regulation kepi. Some still have their blanket rolls of personal effects and most are wearing shell jackets while their Union guards have frock coats. (Library of Congress)

their lives for the benefit of rich planters who had not stirred from their estates. The substitution laws by which rich men could avoid conscription by paying substitutes certainly contributed to this impression. In 1863 there were probably about 100,000 men of military age refusing to serve in the Confederate army and promising to pay a substitute instead.

After Gettysburg the Army of Northern Virginia's already bad reputation for straggling became a good deal worse. Thousands of soldiers absented themselves without leave that autumn but at least most of them returned to the colors for the 1864 campaign. The next year was different and Lee's army withered away at the end of 1864 as many men realized defeat was inevitable. The western parts of North Carolina effectively dropped out of the Confederacy in 1864; deserters, draft-dodgers and Unionists combining to resist the authority of Richmond.

Southern morale sagged after each defeat but it soared after every victory. Even after all hopes of European intervention had gone and large parts of the South had been penetrated by Union forces, the Confederate soldiers were more than willing to fight on. The rise of the anti-war movement in the North and the prospect of Lincoln losing the 1864 election certainly gave grounds for optimism. Lincoln's victory and the fall of Atlanta extinguished these hopes.

PAT CLEBURNE'S CAREER

The meteoric Civil War career of Pat Cleburne began and ended with the infantry, and his fortunes mirrored those of the foot soldiers he led to war. Patrick Ronayne Cleburne began his military career in February 1846, enlisting as a private soldier in Her Majesty's 41st Regiment of Foot. He was 18 years old. By December 1862 he was a major-general in the Confederate Army and his outstanding combat record would lead him to be hailed as "The Stonewall Jackson of the West."

Pat Cleburne was the son of a doctor in County Cork and although he had no great enthusiasm to follow in his father's footsteps, he became an apprentice under a doctor in Mallow. His father died in 1843 but Cleburne persevered with the career chosen for him and applied to a medical school in Dublin. When he failed the entrance

Dulce et decorum est pro patria mori ... The gruesome reality of Civil War battle is mercilessly exposed in this photograph of Confederate dead outside the Union battery at Robinett, Corinth, after Van Dorn's attack on October 4, 1862. Many photographs of Civil War casualties were carefully composed by the photographer and some look so peaceful they could be sleeping. Not here: Colonel William Rogers (left) lies grotesquely exposed with his beard crusted with blood; Colonel Ross (second from left) has a fist-sized exit-hole in his head. Rogers, commander of the 2nd Texas, was shot dead by a Union drummer boy as he personally planted his regiment's colors on the Federal parapet. (Library of Congress)

examination in 1846 he was bitterly disappointed and decided not to return home; he joined the Army instead, selecting the 41st Foot which he believed to be under orders for India.

If he had entertained thoughts of winning martial glory on the plains of the Punjab, he was soon disappointed again. As the dreadful famine engulfed Ireland in the late spring of 1846, the 41st Foot remained in Dublin and provided numerous detachments to maintain order in an increasingly desperate land. Cleburne was an unusual private soldier: he neither drank nor smoked and spent much time in the garrison library studying law and history. In early 1849 as the famine began to pass, the 41st Foot was stationed in Cork, only eight miles from Cleburne's home, and he re-established contact with his family. He was probably not surprised to learn that they were emigrating to America – three years of famine had already driven thousands of Irish people across the Atlantic – and on his 21st birthday that March he received a large enough legacy to purchase his discharge. He was recognized as a promising soldier and was made corporal in July with the prospect of further promotion in future years. But he bought his way out and joined his family for the 50-day voyage from Cork to New Orleans, arriving in the South's largest city on Christmas Day, 1849.

The family went their separate ways in America, Patrick finding work managing a drug store in Helena, Arkansas. He was a diligent young man and within a few years became a partner in the business before turning to law. He became a member of the bar by 1856 and his legal business was flourishing as the fateful election of 1860 approached.

In the summer of 1860 Pat Cleburne became one of the first citizens of Helena to volunteer for the Yell Rifles – named after Archibald Yell, the former governor of Arkansas killed in action at the battle of Buena Vista. Such volunteer units elected their officers, and as one of the few men with any previous military experience Cleburne was elected captain. His reasons for fighting were quite straightforward, as he explained in letters to his family. He had become a leading figure in Helena, active in local politics and as determined as the rest of the community to defend States' rights against Lincoln and the Republicans. He owned no slaves himself and seems to have regarded opposition to slavery as part of a plot to shift the balance of power

Major-General John C. Breckinridge was the US Vice-President 1856–60 and the Southern Democrats' presidential candidate in the fateful 1860 election. He left it until the very last moment to resign from the senate and then proved that not every "political general" was an incompetent. He fought at Shiloh, Murfreesboro, Chickamauga, and Missionary Ridge before managing a very successful campaign in the Shenandoah valley. His victory at New Market was a particular success and the battlefield is preserved to this day. (US National Archives)

away from the agricultural South and toward the industrial North. His attitude to slavery was highly pragmatic as his comrades-in-arms would shortly discover.

In February 1861 Cleburne's company took part in the bloodless seizure of the Federal arsenal at Little Rock. The State Convention held there the following month voted to secede from the Union, while Captain Cleburne spent his days drilling his volunteers and his nights studying military textbooks. On May 14 he was unanimously elected colonel of the regiment now known as the 1st Infantry Regiment of Arkansas Volunteers. There were eight companies armed with Minié rifles and one company with Sharps rifles. Their uniforms were in a poor state after a few months and the assembling Confederate forces in the west were soon struck by a measles epidemic.

Cleburne's regiment took part in the invasion of Kentucky, reaching Bowling Green in October. It belonged to a division of the grandly named Central Army of Kentucky, commanded by none other than William J. Hardee, author of the pre-war *Infantry Tactics* manual. Promoted to major-general, Hardee selected Cleburne to command his 2nd brigade, consisting of the 1st and 5th Arkansas, the 5th Tennessee and the 6th Mississippi regiments.

Cleburne was an enthusiastic and dedicated trainer and his brigade, like the 1st Arkansas regiment, won a high reputation for its drill. By November it was almost entirely equipped with imported British Enfield rifles although the appearance of the men was anything but uniform.

Five months later Cleburne's brigade was heavily engaged at the battle of Shiloh. The 6th

This Confederate infantryman is shown with a blanket roll over a backpack. He carries a cartridge box on his belt and a scabbard for his bayonet. He appears to have tucked his trouser bottoms into his socks. (US National Archives)

Mississippi suffered over 70 percent casualties in the bitter fighting that followed the capture of Sherman's encampment. Cleburne led his brigade with great personal bravery, eventually driving back the Federals on his front. By nightfall he was within 400 yards of Pittsburgh Landing and under fire from Union gunboats as well as field guns. In his report he said he had entered battle with 2,700 men but had only 800 under his command that fateful Sunday night. Hundreds were dead or wounded, but hundreds more had simply vanished, some fleeing in terror while others spent the day looting the enemy camp. Many other battles of the Civil War would have a high proportion of "missing" among the casualties for similar reasons.

In July 1862 Braxton Bragg concentrated the Army of Tennessee for his Kentucky campaign. Cleburne's brigade traveled by railroad from Tupelo, Mississippi, to Chattanooga via Mobile and Atlanta. Bragg temporarily appointed Cleburne to the command of a division but Cleburne was shot in the mouth during the battle of Gibb's Meadow, losing two teeth. He spent several weeks recuperating but rejoined his old brigade, now assigned to Buckner's division – in time for the battle of Perryville. Here he was wounded again, hit in the leg and body while his prized horse "Dixie" was killed under him. A Confederate battery also fired on his brigade by mistake; Cleburne blamed the error on the fact that so many of his men were wearing "blue Federal pants." Confederate regulations called for trousers of a similar hue: but the fact that soldiers wearing them were taken for Yankees suggests that no one in the Army of Tennessee was ever issued with a pair.

Although he left the battlefield on an ambulance cart, Cleburne had impressed his superiors with another successful attack. Hardee, Buckner, and Bragg recommended him for promotion and he was duly commissioned as a major-general in December 1862. Several weeks later at Murfreesboro, his command drove back the Union forces for over three miles in a spectacular assault that routed McCook's Corps.

Marching to join the Army in Virginia, July 1861

A

Arkansas volunteers shooting and drilling, summer 1861

B

Anderson's Brigade in "Bloody Lane," Sharpburg, September 17, 1862

C

The aftermath of battle; a Confederate field hospital

D

Private and 1st lieutenant, Army of Northern Virginia, late 1862

E

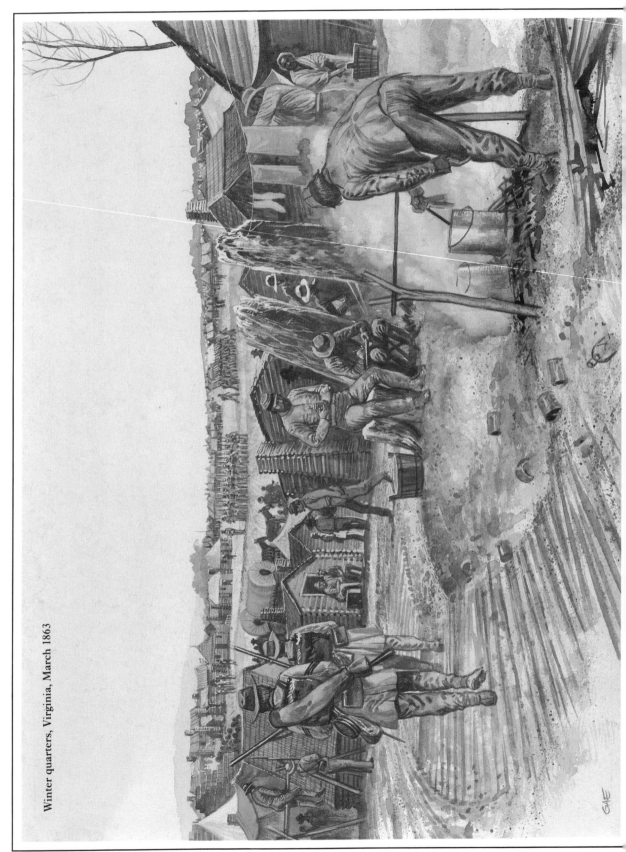

Winter quarters, Virginia, March 1863

F

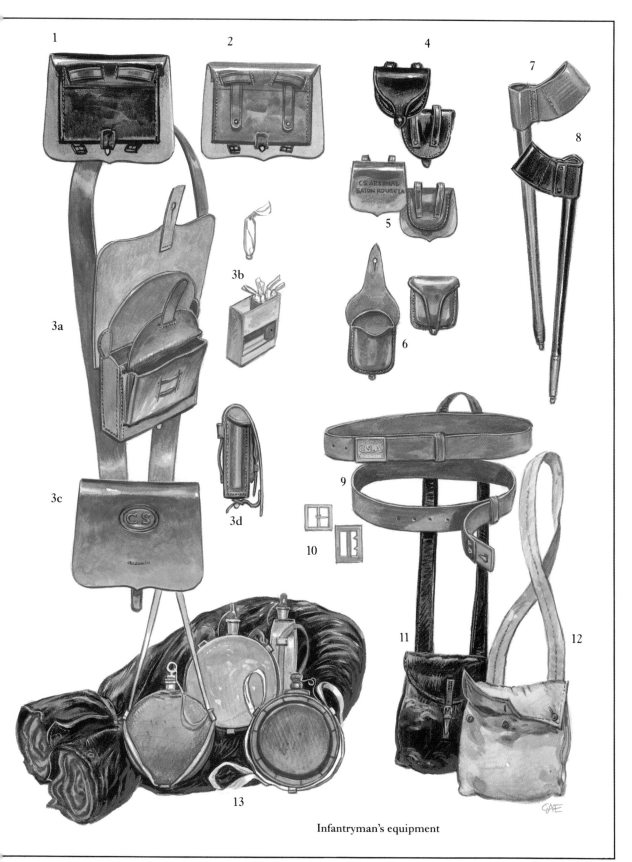

Infantryman's equipment

G

Rifle and personal equipment

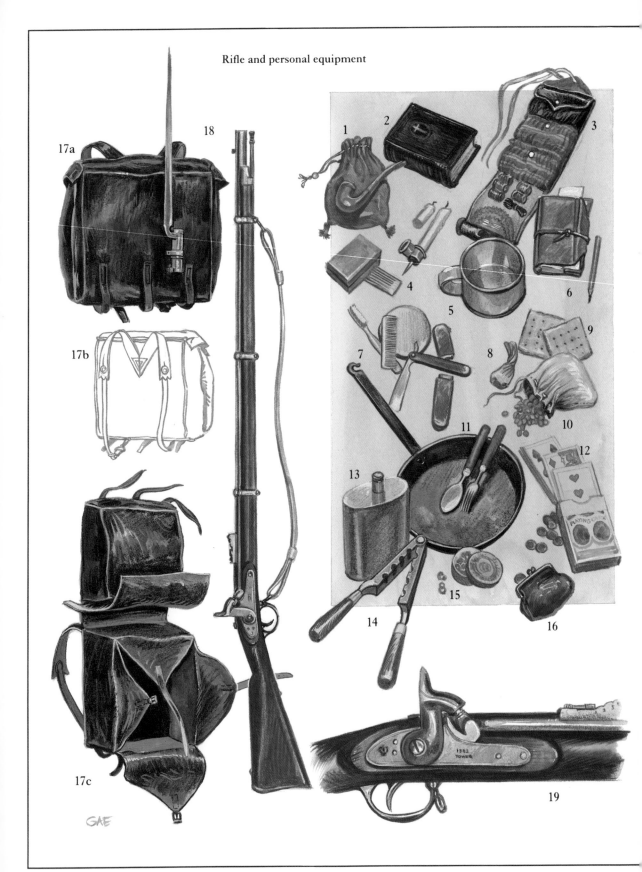

"Devil's Den," Corporal, 1st Texas Infantry,
Gettysburg, July 2, 1863

I

J   The Battle of the Wilderness, May 5, 1864

In the "ditches" at Petersburg, January 1, 1865

K

The retreat from Nashville, Private, Army of Tennessee, December 1864

Manufactured with machinery and parts captured at Harper's Ferry in 1861, the Richmond Armory .58 caliber rifled musket followed the general layout of the US Model 1861. The lock dies seized there were designed for the Maynard Tape Primer system, which was not adopted by the Confederates. This gave the Richmond rifles their characteristic "humpback" lockplates. (Virginia Historical Society)

Confederate skirmishers in action at Culp's Hill, Gettysburg. According to Hardee's *Infantry Tactics*, skirmishers were supposed to fight in four-man subunits he called "comrades in battle" – so the four-man fire teams used by the British and American armies today are not so new as might be thought. (US National Archives)

Before the battle of Perryville, Cleburne had organized a special sharpshooter detachment in his brigade. In early 1863 he secured five English Whitworth sniper rifles, imported at a cost of $1,000 each by the Confederate army. He held a shooting match to select the best five shots in the brigade to shoot them, and they operated as a special sniper unit commanded by a lieutenant. A year later Cleburne secured 30 Whitworths and 15 Kerr rifles – the largest allotment of these expensive weapons made to any Confederate division. The Whitworths came with telescopic sights and fired a mechanically fitting bullet from a hexagonal bore. They are deadly weapons indeed, Cleburne's reports mention his sharpshooters picking off mounted men at up to 1,300 yards!

Cleburne won further laurels at Chickamauga and Chattanooga and it was his division that repulsed Sherman's assault at Missionary Ridge. His well-drilled and highly motivated command had an almost unbroken run of tactical success. It is quite likely that he would have been promoted further but for his initiative of January 1864. Concerned over the growing Union numerical advantage, Cleburne wrote a detailed memorandum arguing for the use of black troops by the South. He had no personal interest nor ideological commitment to slavery, but many other officers did. Of the senior officers of the Army of Tennessee, only Hardee and Hindman were prepared to endorse Cleburne's

proposal; Bragg's reaction was apoplectic. Regarding it as a political rather than military issue, General Joe Johnston refused to pass it on to the War Department and when a copy reached President Davis he ordered it to be suppressed. Cleburne had thought the unthinkable.

If his action cast a cloud over his future career prospects, Cleburne soon had another matter on his mind. In January 1864 his friend General Hardee, a 48-year-old widower married 26-year-old Mary Foreman Lewis in Alabama and Cleburne was his best man. The maid of honor was 24-year-old Susan Tarleton and Cleburne fell in love with her that afternoon. With the army in winter quarters, he was able to visit her in Mobile and they became engaged in March 1864. The plans for their marriage were under way when Johnston was replaced by the fire-eating John Bell Hood and the Army of Tennessee went on to the offensive.

Leaving his fiancée behind, Cleburne joined his division for his final campaign knowing his younger brother Christopher had given his life for the Confederacy. He had joined Morgan's cavalry, staying with Cleburne's division in the winter of 1863 after the abortive raid on Indiana. But in May 1864 he was killed in action at Cloyd's Mountain, Virginia.

Cleburne was dismayed by the manner of Johnston's replacement, and suspicious of Hood's abilities as a General. After the debacle at Spring Hill there is some evidence that he considered arresting the commander of the Army of Tennessee after Schofield's Union corps was allowed to escape from almost certain destruction. However, Cleburne shrank from so drastic an action and led his men up the Columbia Turnpike to Franklin. There they discovered the Union army, now safely ensconced in a line of earthworks with clear fields of fire across the barren landscape. At the council of war that followed, Cleburne recommended a flanking maneuver rather than a frontal assault, but Hood decided otherwise.

At about four o'clock on a bleak November afternoon, Cleburne's division formed into line of battle and marched toward the Union entrenchments alongside Brown's division and most of Stewart's Corps. With no artillery support, the infantry were soon battered by the enemy cannon. The pace quickened, the bands striking up "Dixie" and "The Bonnie Blue Flag." With parade ground precision, Cleburne's division reached the Confederate skirmishers, lying down within a few hundred yards of the enemy outposts. The Union skirmishers slipped away from their rifle pits and fell back to the main defensive position.

Drums beating and flags flying, 15,000 Confederate infantrymen leveled their rifles and charged. Against orders, some of the Union outposts tried to hold their ground and were

The famous Alexander Gardner photograph of a dead Confederate at Devil's Den shows how the infantrymen had built stone *sangars* among the giant boulders. Confederate sharpshooters established in these positions picked off a series of Union officers on the crest of Little Round Top, hitting Major-General Warren and Brigadier-General Weed as well as many regimental officers. (US National Archives)

overrun; as they fled they were so closely pursued by Cleburne's men that the main line was prevented from firing for fear of shooting their own men. For a tantalizing moment it seemed as if Hood's impetuous tactics were going to succeed: the tattered battle flags of the Army of Tennessee were carried over the Union breastworks. The divisions of Cleburne and Brown had broken the enemy center.

It could not last. The Federals had several fresh brigades in hand which launched an immediate counter-attack. Stewart's Corps was driven back and Cleburne's division, stubbornly refusing to surrender the ground won at such cost, were caught in a deadly crossfire. "I never saw men put in such a terrible position as Cleburne's division was for a few minutes," observed a Federal officer who fought at Franklin.

Cleburne's horse, Red Pepper, was killed under him at the beginning of the attack. He mounted another which was killed as his men neared the enemy breastworks, receiving full regimental volleys from the Union defenders before they went into independent fire. He disentangled himself from the saddle and drew his sword. He was last seen waving his hat and shouting encouragement to the leading wave of infantrymen as they poured into the Union position.

His division fought on, even after being driven out of the Union lines. During the night many of Cleburne's men held on in the ditch below the breastworks, unaware of the fate of their commander, but perhaps sensing the absence of leadership. Pat Cleburne was found the next morning, lying about 50 yards short of the Federal earthworks. He had been shot through the heart.

LOGISTICS

The Confederate volunteers of 1861 soon realized that their army's logistic organization left much to be desired. Soldiers throughout the ages have moaned about the kit they are issued or the lack of it and complaints about the rations are a standard feature of military life. The significance of the Confederates' logistic difficulties is that their opponents were extremely well supplied. They enjoyed better food and medical care and were provided with proper clothing. Union infantry regiments had a higher proportion of rifles to start with and few of them had to make do with percussion muskets after 1862. The appearance of breech-loading weapons in large numbers from 1864 gave them a clear advantage on the battlefield.

Sustained by vastly greater industrial resources and supplied by a far more extensive rail network, the Union armies had a clear logistic advantage.

The fact that this was not translated into an early victory does not mean that logistic factors were unimportant: it actually says more about the Union high command. The enigmatic George B. McClellan was a master of organization. A professional soldier turned successful businessman, McClellan provided the Army of the Potomac with probably the best logistic administration of any army either side of the Atlantic. But he was cautious beyond belief; a critical failing ably exploited by Lee.

Confederate infantrymen were supposed to receive the same rations as their Northern opponents. As laid down by the regulations of 1857, these consisted of:

Per man
¾lb pork or bacon or 1¼lb beef (fresh or salt).
18oz bread or flour or 12oz hard bread or 1¼lb of corn bread/corn meal.

Per 100 rations
eight quarts peas or beans or 10lb rice.
6lb coffee.
12lb sugar.
4 quarts vinegar.
two quarts salt.

Unfortunately the quantity and quality of Confederate rations seldom lived up to this standard. The official standards were progressively reduced in 1862 and 1863 and Commissary General Northrop conceded that it proved impossible to supply even the reduced rations for the last two years of the war. While an army was encamped near a railhead supplies could be brought forward; once the army was on the march it was largely on its own. One reason for some Confederate commanders insisting on a rapid rate of march was that it proved easier to supply a fast-moving army. When the troops lingered in the same locality they soon ate all available food stocks. Many campaigns took place in areas which were largely uncultivated and provided little surplus food anyway.

Food shortages affected the health of Confederate soldiers in several ways. Vitamin deficiency from the lack of fresh vegetables led to outbreaks of scurvy and cannot have helped the already low rate of recovery from wounds and diseases. Diarrhea, or the "Mississippi two step," was the bane of many a soldier's life. Their diet of green corn and unripe apples before the battle may well have contributed to the bloody-minded resistance of the Confederate infantry at Antietam. Indeed, the whole 1862 Maryland campaign was dominated by logistic factors: Lee maneuvered his army in several columns, dispersing to live off the land but combining to fight in the classic Napoleonic tradition. Unfortunately, McClellan captured a copy of Lee's orders and sought to defeat the Confederates in detail. If it had been led by a reasonably competent general the Union army would probably have achieved a major victory; even with McClellan in command, it came as close as it ever would to defeating Lee's men in a stand-up fight.

The Confederate logistic effort was undermined in 1862 by the loss of the South's greatest city and manufacturing center, New Orleans. General A.S. Johnston's allowing himself to be maneuvered out of Nashville did not help either. Once Missouri,

Three Confederate soldiers from Pickett's division, photographed by their Union captors on July 7, 1863. They have surrendered their rifles, but retain the rest of their kit including water bottles and tin cups, blanket rolls and knapsacks. Their "uniform" consists of government issue grey/brown trousers, only one of them has on an army jacket, and they all wear slouch hats rather than kepis.

Kentucky, and western Tennessee had fallen, the South lost its best horse-breeding grounds and the shortage of top-quality horses affected the artillery in both main theaters of war. Bragg's counter-offensive that culminated in the battle of Perryville was as heavily influenced by logistic factors as Lee's invasion of Maryland. Unable to recapture Nashville, he marched the Army of Tennessee against Louisville but by September his army was short of everything except firearms. The lack of local volunteers left 15,000 stands of arms unused in the Army wagons.

With worn-out boots and a severe food shortage, the Confederates relied on supplies brought forward from Lexington by wagon. Buell's Union army was able to use parts of the Louisville–Nashville railroad but his forces still had to disperse into separate columns to live off the land. He was unable to exercise close control over each element, hence the confusion at Perryville when the left wing of the Federal army encountered Bragg's Confederates. The tactical victory achieved by the Confederates at Perryville had little strategic impact, once the Union army was fully concentrated it enjoyed a substantial numerical advantage and even the aggressive Bragg saw the wisdom of digging in. However, there were only about two days' rations at the Confederate depot at Bryantsville and the Federals showed no enthusiasm for a frontal assault on the Confederate position. With deep reluctance Bragg ordered a retreat through the Cumberland Gap and that was the end of the campaign. The

Confederate infantry had given a good account of themselves on the battlefield, hungry and footsore as they were. But the opposing Union army was larger, better supplied and led with some measure of confidence.

The Army of Northern Virginia was handicapped by logistic problems throughout its existence. The great defensive victory of Fredericksburg in December 1862 was followed by the incredible Chancellorsville campaign in which the outnumbered Confederates outflanked and outfought General Hooker's reorganized Union army. But this stunning tactical triumph could not be followed up because the Army of Northern Virginia had a desperate shortage of horses and could not supply itself unless it remained close to Richmond. The Confederacy was using up horses faster than it could breed them: mostly to illnesses brought on by their poor diet. This affected the infantrymen just as well as the cavalry or artillery since all soldiers depended on horse-drawn supply wagons.

Lee had to wait until enough spring forage, vegetables and grain-fed cattle could be obtained before he could launch his second invasion of the North. The subsequent Gettysburg campaign was strongly influenced by logistics, the army again living off the land in the classic Napoleonic manner. The battle itself was brought on by troops heading for the town of Gettysburg because it was thought to have a plentiful supply of shoes. After the withdrawal to Virginia, the following Mine Run

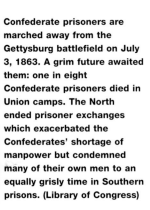

Confederate prisoners are marched away from the Gettysburg battlefield on July 3, 1863. A grim future awaited them: one in eight Confederate prisoners died in Union camps. The North ended prisoner exchanges which exacerbated the Confederates' shortage of manpower but condemned many of their own men to an equally grisly time in Southern prisons. (Library of Congress)

Lt-Gen James Longstreet, Lee's "Old Warhorse," graduated from West Point in 1842 and fought in the Mexican War. As a Major-General, he commanded one half of the Army of Northern Virginia while Jackson commanded the other but his career suffered a serious reverse at Gettysburg. Longstreet's torpid pace of advance seriously delayed the attack on Devil's Den/Little Round Top on the second day. At Chickamauga he staged one of the most concentrated infantry attacks ever made by the Confederates, breaking the Union army in two. (US National Archives)

campaign was equally dominated by supply problems – especially the horse shortage which was exacerbated by an outbreak of the disease glanders.

After his soldiers had driven the Army of the Potomac back over the Rappahannock in the fall of 1863, Robert E. Lee wrote to Secretary Seddon explaining the difficulties facing the ordinary infantry. Many were barefoot and few men had overcoats, blankets or warm clothing. Although he described his men's cheerfulness in adversity as "the sublimest sight of the war," Lee was forced to cease active campaigning and go into winter quarters. The Confederate logistic organization could supply his army if it remained near Richmond, but not if he advanced against Meade. Lee's offensive strategy had at last been checked, not by enemy action but by logistical limitations.

The railroad

The Confederates' success in exploiting the newfound mobility conferred by the railroad has been touched on above. Their impressive strategic concentrations in the Shiloh and Chattanooga campaigns were achieved over a rail network that gradually disintegrated during the course of the war. By 1864 the railroads were in a poor state of repair and unable to transport enough goods for military or civilian use. Thus some parts of the Confederacy suffered dreadful food shortages while others had surplus crops that could not be moved.

The deterioration of the railroads might have been inevitable given the loss of so much

Disposal of the dead presented a major problem to the armies of the Civil War: neither side had anticipated the sheer number of casualties. On several battlefields, many bodies remained unburied for months. At Gettysburg the cemetery was only a quarter completed by the time of Lincoln's address – the local contractor hired by the State of Pennsylvania could only bury 100 a day. He charged $1.59 each. (US National Archives)

Confederate guerrillas fire on Union steamboats on the Mississippi. The Union army ordered the construction of armored gunboats in 1861 and the superior industrial resources of the North produced a larger and more powerful river fleet than the South could construct. The Mississippi became a key Union invasion and supply route and, with the fall of Vicksburg in 1863, it cut Texas and Arkansas off from the rest of the Confederacy. (US National Archives)

THE CIVIL WAR IN AMERICA : JEFFERSON THOMPSON'S GUERRILLAS SHOOTING AT FEDERAL BOATS ON THE MISSISSIPPI.—FROM A SKETCH BY OUR SPECIAL ARTIST.—[SEE PAGE 350.

manufacturing capability, but they might have been better maintained if the Confederate government had taken greater interest in controlling them. The Confederate rail network was not just smaller than that of the Union: it was never run as efficiently either. A bill was proposed in the Confederate Congress as early as 1861, proposing government regulation of the railroads for military purposes. The railroad owners managed to get it buried in committee by their political allies and were free to run the rail network for their own profit, regardless of the military consequences. In April 1863, with the Army of Northern Virginia suffering from a critical shortage of food, Congress granted the President the authority to control the railroads. At last the War Department rather than the railroad owners could decide which goods had priority; it could also enable rolling stock from one railroad to be used on another. Sad to relate, Congress then sabotaged the measure by failing to confirm the office of railroad superintendent. The railroads carried on as before.

Medical services

Like many aspects of the Civil War, the medical services were a mixture of old and new. The Confederates formed an infirmary corps in 1862,

following the Union lead, and the widespread use of chloroform meant that grim Napoleonic scenes of men having to bite their belts while surgeons operated without anaesthetic were mercifully few. One happy by-product of Jackson's valley campaign was the capture of 15,000 cases of chloroform.[15] Before a major battle the companies of each infantry regiment would detail a small squad of men to take the wounded to the rear where field hospitals would be established, either in nearby houses or under canvas. These battlefield infirmaries were organized at brigade level with the surgeons from each regiment working together. The wounded were assessed as they were brought in: the more lightly wounded would be treated on the spot, and the more seriously injured evacuated to the field hospitals. The most urgent cases were operated on immediately then sent back on ambulance carts. From the field hospitals they would eventually be transferred to general hospitals in the cities.

Unfortunately for the Confederate infantryman, this basically sound system often failed him. The sheer number of wounded produced by Civil War battles often overwhelmed the available medical

---

15. McPHERSON, James M. *The Battle Cry of Freedom* Oxford 1988

Joseph E. Johnston became a full General in the Confederate army in 1861 and commanded the forces defending Richmond against McClellan's advance from the Peninsula. He had lost effective control of the campaign by the time he was wounded at Seven Pines and replaced by Lee. He did better as commander of the Army of Tennessee, conducting a masterful Fabian strategy that delayed the fall of Atlanta for months. He died of a chill in 1891, contracted at the funeral of his respected opponent William T. Sherman. (US National Archives)

facilities: this was especially true of the major battles of 1862 when the scale of casualties was a surprise to everyone. After Shiloh the city of Corinth was crammed with wounded men, many dying slowly, painfully and unnecessarily. Richmond was just the same two months later in the wake of the Seven Days' campaign.

Throughout the war there were never enough trained medical staff available. The need for doctors was so acute that many unqualified men were hired on the understanding that they would take their examinations in due course. Soldiers were understandably dubious about the talents of even the qualified staff since mid-19th-century medicine was a haphazard business at best.

Surgeons washed neither their hands nor their clothes between operations, and although some rinsed their instruments, the idea of sterilizing them would not occur until after the war. Gangrene could set in even with minor wounds, and amputation was the only answer. A gunshot wound in the stomach was invariably fatal as there was no contemporary treatment for peritonitis.

Disease

Despite the heavy casualties suffered on the battlefields, two to three times as many soldiers died of disease than by enemy action. More Confederate infantrymen were laid in their graves by typhoid, smallpox or dysentery than by Yankee bullets. Ironically, in view of the Confederates' dim views of city-dwellers, recruits from the rural South were far more vulnerable than volunteers from the towns. The country boys were physically fit but they had not been exposed to so many diseases and consequently had no immunity.

The Confederates did not help themselves by their own insanitary practices when in camp. Already affected by a poor diet, thousands of soldiers became ill because their water supply was polluted. Even on meager rations, a single infantry regiment would deposit 400 lbs of excrement per day and unless sanitary arrangements were well organized there was a significant health risk. Newspapermen reporting from Corinth after Shiloh said the water smelt so bad you had to hold your nose to drink it. Latrines were known to the Confederates as "sinks" and even when they were dug, officers had to work hard to make the men actually use them. All too many soldiers would relieve themselves against the nearest tree. There was very little soap and the nearest many soldiers came to washing was marching in the rain. Everyone had fleas.

Flies were a perennial problem but the mosquitoes were worse. From April to October they plagued Confederate encampments, causing fevers which were usually attributed to "bad air" from swampy ground. Malaria was a very common disease and it was predictably most severe along the coast of South Carolina, Georgia, and Florida. Typhoid was less common, but about one in four soldiers that contracted it died. The worst outbreak took place in the Confederate army in Virginia in 1861, when the greatest concentration of young men from isolated rural areas took place. Typhoid diminished after 1862 and was unheard of by the end of the war. However, another disagreeable consequence of the invasion of Maryland in 1862 was an outbreak of smallpox. Some cases were reported in the Army of the Potomac before the campaign but a major epidemic followed in Virginia, lasting until the spring of 1863. Confederate infantrymen also suffered from scurvy, bronchitis, and pneumonia; a few soldiers in most regiments became infected with venereal diseases and cures for them were widely advertised in Richmond newspapers.

Confederate casualties

The precise number of Confederate casualties was never known during the war, and cannot be established now. Surviving Confederate records make it equally unclear exactly how many men served in the Southern armies.

Estimates of the Confederate forces range from approximately 600,000 to 1.4 million with most historians accepting a figure of around 750,000. The most exhaustive studies of Confederate losses suggest that 250,000 men gave their lives for the South: a terribly high proportion.

THE PLATES

A: Marching to join the Army in Virginia, July 1861

The wave of patriotic fervor which swept the Confederacy in the early weeks of the war saw men of all ages flocking to the colors. Great crowds gathered in every town to see the local militia march off to the front, convinced that the Yankees would be whipped and the war over in a matter of weeks.

The army that assembled in Richmond in 1861 wore no single regulation uniform, each militia regiment arriving in its pre-war finery. Here a well-equipped regiment of a large town somewhere in the Carolinas musters at the local rail depot prior to leaving for Richmond. Apart from the havelocks and gaiters there is little standardization in the uniforms of each company. The officers wear a modified version of the pre-war uniform of the US regular army. The youthful lieutenant in the foreground holds an early version of the "Stars and Bars" national flag. It was not unusual for these to have been hand stitched by the ladies of the town and presented to the regiment often with a dedication stitched into the flag. In the background, amid the tearful farewells of wives and

Confederate prisoners-of-war seen at Chattanooga, November 1863. At that time the city was under effective siege by Confederate forces after Rosecrans' defeat. Some of the men are still wearing overcoats they had captured from Union soldiers in happier times. (Library of Congress)

sweethearts, an officer gives travel instructions to a group of sergeants whose job it will be to maintain some degree of order on the march. Some of the officers have brought family slaves with them but most of these will be sent home before the end of the year.

B: Arkansas volunteers shooting and drilling, summer 1861

Though few of the men that joined the Confederate infantry in 1861 were strangers to firearms, the mechanics of army drill were a mystery to the vast majority. Recruits tended to come from rural communities in which most households had guns and many either hunted for food or shot vermin on their farms. The degree of formal training varied wildly, the chief objective being to teach the soldiers to maneuver in formation. Some commanders such as Jackson insisted on regular drill, but this was the exception rather than the rule. Most units took a very relaxed attitude to drill and very few reached the level of expertise demanded by Jackson. This lack of enthusiasm for drill became increasingly prevalent later in the war. Many officers, particularly in remote areas, had little or no training themselves.

The little training that did take place was organized, as here, by officers. This plantation owner is using a newly acquired drill book to instruct volunteers from his county – a mixture of

local farm boys with one or two regular army veterans. What little experience these "veterans" have will mark them out for early promotion.

While many farmhands had only ever fired shotguns or small-caliber squirrel guns, there were certainly some excellent marksmen in the Confederate infantry. Shooting competitions were organized, although these were rather different from modern target shooting. Instead of engaging large targets from several hundred yards, they fired at one-inch-square paper patches at about 50 yards. Each man had a fixed number of shots, usually about a dozen. It was not unknown for riflemen to put all 12 rounds through the one-inch target.

C: Anderson's Brigade in "Bloody Lane," Sharpsburg, September 17, 1862

The center of the Confederate line at Sharpsburg (Antietam) rested on a sunken road that was dubbed "The Bloody Lane" after the terrible slaughter that occurred there during the battle. It was initially defended by Rodes' Alabama Brigade, deployed (west to east) in the order 26th, 12th, 3rd, 4th, and 5th Regiments. The line was continued by the 2nd, 14th, 4th, and 30th Regiments of Anderson's North Carolina Brigade. The combined strength of these two brigades was about 1,900 men.

The lane lay in dead ground, a gentle crest about 150 yards in front of the position hiding it from the view of the Union lines. Skirmishers posted on the

A "skulker" is intercepted by a watchful NCO during the battle of Fair Oaks, 1862. Although the Confederate army did employ the death penalty for desertion, such men had to be persistent offenders or just very unlucky to end up sitting on a coffin facing a firing party. (US National Archives)

crest fell back at about 9.00 a.m. under pressure from Brig.Gen. Max Weber's Brigade, part of French's division of the Union II Corps, which was advancing in close-order line with no skirmish screen. The 900-man 1st Delaware Regiment on its own outnumbered the entire Alabama brigade. The Confederate opening volley, fired at about 20 yards, destroyed this massive formation at a stroke, and Anderson's brigade drove off the 5th Maryland and 4th New York in similar style, the latter losing 187 out of 450 men in a matter of minutes.

In the assaults that followed the Federal troops established themselves on the crest and Southern losses mounted. Repeated Union attacks were hurled against the defenders of "Bloody Lane" all morning. John B. Gordon, commander of the 6th Alabama Regiment, and a future general, had sworn to Lee that his men would hold the lane until the sun went down, but the Confederates had no reserves. The Alabama Brigade suffered over 40 percent casualties, standing its ground against apparently limitless numbers of Yankees. Gordon was himself shot through his left arm, left shoulder and right leg (twice), before finally collapsing with a bullet in the face. He fell with his face in his kepi and could have drowned in his own blood, if an earlier near miss had not drilled a neat hole in his cap.

"Bloody Lane" was finally stormed at about 1.00 pm by a well-coordinated Union attack after a battery of 12-pdr. "Napoleons" had been brought forward to enfilade the position.

D: The aftermath of battle; a Confederate field hospital

There was roughly one doctor for every 324 men in the Southern armies. The massive number of casualties resulting from any major battle instantly overwhelmed the medical facilities of both sides, but Confederate field hospitals were further handicapped by their small staffs and chronic shortage of drugs. Military medicine had improved

considerably since the Napoleonic wars. Pain-killing opiates were in widespread use, and chloroform was available as an anaesthetic – a huge step from the shot of hard liquor and leather tongue strap. Ether and laudanum were also used, but in the latter part of the war the Union blockade drove up the price of drugs in the Confederacy, and many men had to undergo surgery without any form of anaesthetic.

The large-caliber lead bullets of the Civil War inflicted horrific injuries that doctors were usually unable to treat. Shattered limbs were amputated with such frequency that piles of them were visible outside the hospital tents after major actions. Anyone shot in the stomach was left to die; it was impossible to treat this sort of wound effectively.

This Alfred R. Ward drawing depicts a Confederate deserter. The ranks of the Confederate army were constantly depleted by desertion, especially after heavy defeats. Many men left without leave to visit their families and returned when they were ready. Others absented themselves permanently, patting their rifles menacingly if an officer asked where their pass was. Parts of some states became virtually controlled by deserters and draft dodgers. (Library of Congress)

John Bell Hood was one of the South's most controversial officers. His Texas brigade came to notice in the Army of Northern Virginia, attacking with conspicuous courage at Gaines Mill in 1862. Personally fearless, Hood suffered severe injuries to his arm at Gettysburg and had a leg amputated after Chickamauga. He was only 33 when he replaced Joe Johnston in command of the Army of Tennessee. Sherman asked his staff what they should make of their new opponent, and one man reported seeing Hood play poker – he had bet $2,500 with only a pair in his hand. His military strategy and his card playing seem to have had a great deal in common. (US National Archives)

Head wounds were treated similarly, although about one in four men managed to survive. Sepsis was yet to be discovered and doctors did not sterilize their instruments between patients. They probed wound after wound without cleaning their hands and even minor wounds could prove fatal as a result of infection.

The horrors of the field hospitals are vividly described in the letters sent home by soldiers at the front, but there was another terror which doctors were even less able to deal with. Diseases such as measles, typhoid, typhus, and dysentery spread like wildfire amid the filth and squalor of campaign life. Many Southerners from rural communities had never had any contact with such diseases and had little or no immunity. Many more Confederate soldiers succumbed to disease than to Federal bullets.

E: Private and 1st lieutenant, Army of Northern Virginia, late 1862

The Virginian private in the foreground wears the white crossbelts and black-trimmed grey which infantry from the "Old Dominion" continued to wear well into the war. His shell jacket and trousers are the regulation pale grey though Confederate "gray" cloth could be any shade from off-white to dark grey with tinges of green or blue. The yellowy-brown shade often referred to as "Butternut" was also common. Southern infantrymen often supplemented their uniforms with captured Union clothing. After the battle of Shiloh in which large quantities of Union equipment had been captured, the commanders of the Army of Tennessee issued orders banning the men from wearing Federal uniforms. The frequent repetition of these instructions suggests that the men were not complying. This was a habit common to most Confederate soldiers throughout the war. In addition thousands of captured Federal uniforms were bleached or dyed and reissued. Any resemblance between the resulting colors and Confederate dress regulations must have been entirely coincidental. This could make recognition on the battlefield extremely difficult.

The private wears the grey trousers almost universal in the Southern armies. Although Confederate regulations called for sky blue trousers, several accounts described Southern units wearing them being fired upon by their comrades, who automatically associated blue pants with Yankees. This individual has procured a Union haversack and some biscuits; the infamous "Hardtack."

The 1st lieutenant in the background wears the full regulation uniform including the two collar bars and single Austrian knot on his sleeve. Most junior officers' dress was almost indistinguishable from that of their men, the appearance of regulation dress being unusual enough to draw comments in memoirs and diaries. Some individuals did however succeed in turning out in full dress until the end of the war.

F: Winter quarters, Virginia, March 1863

Neither side attempted serious campaigning during the winter months. The unmetalled roads of 19th-century America were turned into quagmires by the rains and even the best-equipped force could find its progress grinding to a halt. The Army of the Potomac's disastrous "mud march" of January 1863 only resulted in further demoralizing the Union troops and lost General Burnside his command. Armies normally went into winter quarters and waited out the worst of the weather; by March the roads had usually dried sufficiently for campaigning to resume.

Here the Army of Northern Virginia has been encamped for several months. The surrounding countryside has been stripped of trees in order to build cabins, fuel campfires and to corduroy the paths in the camp with logs. The soldier sitting astride the narrow beam on the far left is being punished – a symptom of the deterioration in discipline common during the long and boring months of life in camp. Officers attempted to prevent their men from getting up to mischief by filling their time with duties; for example unit drill (as shown in the background, in this case drill by companies). In the foreground two soldiers are returning from picket duty, another regular chore. Judging by the high quality of their uniforms and equipment their unit has recently been re-equipped from army stores.

Piles of stores are visible in the left background. To feed an army on even the meager army rations meant issuing literally tons of food a day. In addition weapons, ammunition, uniforms, and all the necessities of life for an army would need to be supplied and stored. The Confederate logistic system was only able to supply the army properly when it was static and near a railhead. The opportunity could then be taken to make repairs and, where possible, to replace old equipment.

The camps were constructed by the soldiers themselves and, lacking the plentiful supplies of tents provided for their Union opponents, men had to improvise. Where enough timber was available they built pioneer-style log cabins. Otherwise they relied on combinations of brickwork, mud, sticks, and canvas shelters.

G: Infantryman's equipment

G1: M1842 cartridge box.

G2: Confederate copy of M1855 cartridge box in russet leather.

G3a: Open showing front pouch which would hold patches, cleaning rags and musket tools. The rear pouch held two tin containers.

b: Tin container which held 20 rounds, ten vertically on top and a further ten wrapped in a paper package underneath.

c: Buckled, showing flap with stamped "CS" badge.

d: Side view showing arrangements of buckles.

G4: Copy of black leather US Army percussion cap

A Confederate infantryman from Ewell's Corps killed in action at Spotsylvania Court House, May 18, 1864. Ewell's men were attacked at dawn by the Union Corps of Hancock and Wright but the Confederates, fighting from rapidly constructed earthworks, repulsed the assaults. Meade called off further attacks and Grant ordered another outflanking march to begin the next day. (Library of Congress)

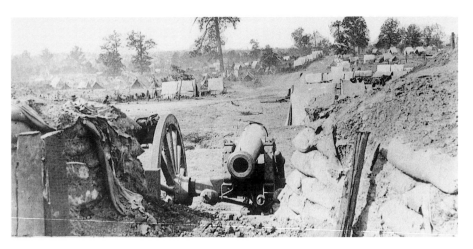

A 12-pounder Napoleon smoothbore in one of the Confederate redoubts protecting Atlanta in 1864. The Napoleon was the most widely used field gun of the war, more effective than rifled guns in the wooded and broken terrain that often dominated Civil War battlefields. Over 630 Napoleons were made in the Confederacy and 1,157 in the North. (US National Archives)

box. The straps on the back are riveted and stitched. A strip of woolly sheepskin was glued and sewed to the back of the pouch at the mouth to prevent caps falling out.

G5: Russet leather cap box from the Confederate arsenal at Baton Rouge. The flap has a separate narrow leather strap sewn on which buttons to the brass finial.

G6: Confederate-made copy of imported British cap box.

G7: Southern-made bayonet scabbard with frog sewn to the scabbard.

G8: Southern copy of US bayonet scabbard for the M1855 rifled musket. The scabbard is stitched to the frog rather than riveted, however.

G9: Russet leather belts were more common than black leather, although many Southerners acquired black Union Army belts. The belt plate is of Southern-made brass, the heavy concentration of copper in the alloy giving it a red coloring.

G10: Frame buckles were more common with the Army of Northern Virginia with belt plates being found more in the Western theaters, particularly amongst the Army of Tennessee. The type on the right is a "Georgia" buckle, with two prongs cast as part of the frame.

G11: The tar-covered US model haversack was relatively waterproof and more popular than Confederate-manufactured models.

G12: This haversack made of white duck with three pewter buttons was the model in use from the beginning of the 19th century until the 1850s.

G13: A variety of blankets were used including captured US Army blankets, civilian blankets, and Army-issued items. These were usually wrapped in a captured US Army issue "gum blanket." These were waterproofed by coating cotton with black rubber and the South was not able to produce such items itself. The canteens are (left to right) a captured wool-covered US Army canteen, two views of a Southern-made tin canteen and a wooden "barrel" type.

H: Rifle and personal equipment

H1–H16 are personal items and would probably have been carried in the haversack or blanket roll.

H1: Pipe and tobacco

H2: Bible

H3: "Housewife" – needle, thread, etc.

H4: Matches and candle

H5: Tin cup

H6: Diary, letters and writing materials

H7: Shaving kit, comb, and toothbrush

H8: A small paper bag of salt

H9: Hardtack biscuits were notoriously inedible and would crack teeth if not soaked in water before eating. They were often broken up with a knife handle or the butt of a gun and fried in bacon fat.

H10: Peanuts or "Goober peas"

H11: Frying pan, fork, and spoon

H12: Playing cards

H13: Can of black powder

H14: Bullet mold

H15: Tin of percussion caps

H16: Purse. Coinage was often carried, though Confederate bills were almost valueless.

H17: The M1853 black leather knapsack

a: back or visible face

b: front showing arrangement of shoulder straps

c: In theory an overcoat was supposed to be

strapped in the bottom section and a clean set of clothes kept in the top. The knapsack was then folded and buckled with three leather straps. In reality the overcoat was rapidly discarded and the knapsack would have been used to carry extra food, spare powder and ammunition, and perhaps a clean shirt and spare socks.

H18: British P1853 Enfield rifle and bayonet
H19: The major English supplier was the London Armoury as indicated by the "TOWER" stamp on the lock of this .577 caliber Enfield rifle.

I: "Devil's Den," Corporal, 1st Texas Infantry, Gettysburg, July 2, 1863

On the afternoon of July 2 this rocky outcrop at the southern end of Houck's Ridge was held by a large brigade of Union Infantry including the 2nd US Sharpshooters. When Longstreet's much delayed assault was launched Law's and Robertson's Brigades were ordered to take the position. Attacking just after 4.00 p.m. the majority of the Confederates attacked Little Round Top, and only the 1st Texas and 3rd Arkansas made directly for Devil's Den. Forced to take cover in the woods northwest of the rocks they engaged the Union defenders for over two hours before finally breaking into the position with the help of a second wave of Confederates – Benning's and Anderson's Brigades.

Amidst the jumble of rocks the regiments became disorganized and the soldiers had to fight in small groups or even individually – a circumstance that suited the average Southern soldier perfectly. They spent the remaining hours of daylight sniping at the Union defenders of nearby

Soldiers of the Army of Northern Virginia during the 1864 campaign, one of the few pictures of Southern troops in F.T. Miller's photographic history of the Civil War produced in 1911. These men were taken prisoner during the battles of May and June in which they inflicted catastrophic casualties on their opponents. (Library of Congress)

Little Round Top, keeping the Yankees pinned down; many officers were picked off, silhouetted against the skyline.

In this scene the Confederates have just flushed the last Federal troops from the Devil's Den and this corporal still has his bayonet fixed. He has acquired an additional cartridge box and is peering toward Little Round Top searching for a target for his Enfield rifle. Unusually he wears rank chevrons. In the small Southern units all the men knew each other, and many NCOs neglected to wear rank badges.

J: The Battle of the Wilderness, May 5, 1864

On May 4, 1864, General U.S. Grant launched the Army of the Potomac on its last great offensive. Like General Hooker at Chancellorsville he hoped to outflank the Army of Northern Virginia. He marched into the densely forested area known as the Wilderness in an attempt to turn the entrenched Confederate position at Mine Run and force a fight in open country. The similarities with Gen. Joseph Hooker's disastrous campaign end there.

Despite the odds, Lee concentrated his army for what was to be its last effective counter-attack. On May 5 the leading elements of the Army of Northern Virginia halted the Federal advance well short of open country. In the thick undergrowth it was not immediately apparent that the Confederates were outnumbered nearly two-to-one. The battle raged until nightfall on May 6 and it was remembered with a particular horror by the survivors on both sides. In the gloomy thickets it was difficult to distinguish friend from foe. General Longstreet was badly wounded by fellow Confederates only a few miles from the sport where Stonewall Jackson was killed in similarly tragic circumstances at Chancellorsville. It was all but impossible to exercise tactical control over a regiment, let alone larger formations. In places the dry undergrowth caught fire, dooming many wounded men to be burnt alive. An infantryman from a South Carolina regiment recalled how he and his comrades pulled several Union soldiers to safety, "all we cared for was that he was a human being and a brother, though we had fought him hard all day." For the Confederates there was at least one advantage in fighting in the Wilderness: the Union army could not exploit its enormous superiority in artillery.

Lee's army sustained 10,000 casualties in the Wilderness, but Union losses were nearly 18,000. Grant, however, did not retreat. He was determined to fight to the finish. From nightfall on May 6 until the last shots near Appomattox 11 months later, Lee's army was locked in a fatal struggle with a vastly stronger enemy.

K: In the "ditches" at Petersburg, January 1, 1865

It snowed on New Year's Day 1865, freezing as far south as Memphis. In the lines of "ditches" (as the soldiers called them) that stretched for over 30 miles around Richmond and Petersburg, the Army of Northern Virginia was holding out to the bitter end. Inadequately dressed against the winter, the men were also short of supplies of every kind; the Southern railway system had all but collapsed. While the army had often been short of shells for the field guns, this was the first time small arms ammunition had to be rationed. To Lee's fury, Southern senators continued to live in conspicuous comfort in Richmond while his soldiers were close to starvation.

Here the arrival of a newspaper offers little comfort to these veterans. While they have been locked in trench warfare against Grant's overwhelming forces, the news from other fronts has been extremely discouraging. Atlanta has fallen, Lincoln has been re-elected and the Army of Tennessee has been shattered at the twin battles of Franklin and Nashville. Confederate currency is virtually worthless, the government fueling inflation by printing more paper money, while Federal presses swamp the country with counterfeit notes to add to the confusion. Prices are now, on average, 28 times their 1861 levels. This hardly matters to the soldiers, however, as their meager pay is erratic.

Killed in the final round: a dead Confederate infantryman at Petersburg. At 4.30 a.m., Sunday April 2, 1865, the Union forces that had besieged Petersburg since the fall attacked all along the line. The overstretched Confederate line collapsed, forcing Lee to withdraw and the Confederate government to evacuate Richmond. General A.P. Hill was among the Confederate dead in the battle that began the final phase of the war. This infantryman had his blanket roll protected from the elements by a captured US waterproof. (Library of Congress)

The regimental commander is the only man here to have an overcoat. Few private soldiers bothered to retain their coats during summer as they were a bulky and unnecessary luxury. They would usually be able to loot one from the Yankees before winter set in. From the autumn of 1864, however, the Army of Northern Virginia was locked in grim trench warfare with their Federal opponents. This continued throughout the winter until the final collapse at the beginning of April 1865. In the trenches the opportunities to "liberate" clothing were minimal and many Confederates shivered through the winter in thin cotton uniforms. One unfortunate, weakened by poor food and disease, has succumbed to exposure. He has already been stripped of his boots to equip one of his comrades and will be buried when the ground thaws.

In the background is a Coehorn mortar, used by both sides at Petersburg. Weighing 164 lbs it fired a 24lb bomb to a maximum range of 1,200 yards. Carefully aimed and with high-quality powder, it could drop its bomb with remarkable accuracy.

L: The retreat from Nashville, Private, Army of Tennessee, December 1864

After the defeat at Nashville the Army of Tennessee retreated for ten days and nights, fighting a succession of rearguard actions. Hood's exhausted soldiers finally crossed the river Tennessee on December 24 and 25; a grim Christmas indeed.

Here one of Hood's soldiers marches along the icy road, his feet wrapped in strips of cloth. The army marched 500 miles in six weeks and its line of retreat was said to have been marked by bloody footprints. The shortage of footwear was so acute that when Bedford Forrest asked for a brigade of infantry to support his cavalry rearguard, many men arrived barefoot. He organized his new mixed command with barefoot infantry riding in wagons and dismounting only when the Union forces approached. Overall, about half of Hood's surviving infantrymen had to hobble southwards with lacerated feet. Food and ammunition were in equally short supply, the Army's logistic system had all but collapsed, and there was little forage available in the barren countryside.

When the army reassembled at Tupelo, Mississippi, General Beauregard was stunned at the pitiful appearance of the men. Gaunt and hollow-eyed, they were a shadow of the once proud army Hood had launched northwards in November. Hood was relieved of his post and his long-suffering army divided. Four thousand journeyed south to join the defenders of Mobile; the rest, approximately 12,000 of all arms, turned east, marching for the Carolinas and what they knew would be the final campaign of the war. It was a column of these men that Mary Chesnut saw passing through Richmond on their way to join the Army of Northern Virginia. They still marched with a jaunty step and were singing as they went. They were soldiers from the indomitable corps of General Stephen D. Lee.

BIBLIOGRAPHY

Richard E. Berringer, Herman Hattaway, Archer Jones & William N. Sill, Jr, *The Elements of Confederate Defeat* (Georgia, 1988)

Clarence Buel & Robert Johnson (eds.), *Battles and Leaders of the Civil War* (New York, 1888)

Brig. Gen. Silas Casey, *Infantry Tactics* (Washington, 1862)

A dead Confederate lies in the spring rain at Petersburg, April 1865. Contested earthworks were often choked with bodies after an infantry assault but at Petersburg most Confederate redoubts surrendered with little more than token resistance. (US National Archives)

Bruce Catton, *The Centennial History of the Civil War* (New York, 1961-65)

Joshua L. Chamberlain, *The Passing of the Armies. An Account of the Final Campaign of the Army of the Potomac. Based on Personal Reminiscences of the Fifth Army Corps* (New York, 1915)

Henry S. Commager, *The Blue & the Gray* (Indianapolis, 1950)

William C. Davis, *The Battle of New Market* (Louisiana, 1975)

Clifford Dowdey, *The Seven Days: The Emergence of Lee* (Wilmington, 1988)

Clifford Dowdey, *Lee's Last Campaign* (North Carolina, 1988)

Ian C. Drury, *The US Civil War Military Machine: weapons and tactics of the Union and Confederate armed forces* (London, 1993)

Norm Flayderman, *Flayderman's Guide to Antique American Firearms, 4th edition* (Northbrook, Illinois, 1987)

Shelby Foote, *The Civil War: A Narrative* (New York, 1958-75)

Edward Hagerman, *The American Civil War and the origins of modern warfare* (Indianapolis, 1992)

Frank A. Haskell, *The Battle of Gettysburg* (London, 1959)

Herman Hattaway & Archer Jones, *How the North Won* (Illinois, 1983)

Lt.Col. G.F.R. Henderson, *Stonewall Jackson and the American Civil War* (London, 1903)

Stanley Horn, *The Army of Tennessee* (Indianapolis, 1941)

Thomas L. Livermore, *Numbers & losses in the Civil War in America* (Boston, 1902)

An Alfred Ward sketch of Former Confederate soldiers taking the Oath at Richmond after the surrender. Two of the men have the almost universal blanket roll but the soldier second from left still retains a backpack. Waterbottles and knapsacks are also shown together with typically battered slouch hats. (Library of Congress)

James L. McDonough, *Shiloh – In Hell before night* (The University of Tennessee Press, 1977)

James M. McPherson, *The Battle Cry of Freedom* (Oxford, 1988)

Grady McWhiney & Perry Jamieson, *Attack and Die, Civil War military tactics and the Southern Heritage* (Alabama, 1982)

Francis T. Miller (ed.), *The Photographic History of the Civil War* (New York, 1911)

James V. Murfin, *The Gleam of Bayonets* (1965)

Maj. Henry T. Osterhoudt, *Towards Organized Disorder: The evolution of American infantry assault tactics 1778-1919*, unclassified DTIC technical report (Alexandria, 1979)

John M. Priest, *Antietam: The Soldier's Battle* (Pennsylvania, 1989)

Col. H.C.B. Rogers, *Confederates and Federals at war* (London, 1973)

Bell Irwin Wiley, *The Life of Johnny Reb* (Indianapolis, 1943)

Periodicals

The American Rifleman, the official journal of the National Rifle Association of America

Civil War Times Illustrated

John B. Gordon was a lawyer before the war and had no prior military experience. But he proved a capable and dependable officer, winning promotion to brigadier-general by November 1862 and finishing the war as a major-general commanding Jackson's old corps. It was Gordon's heavy duty to lead the Army of Northern Virginia to the final surrender ceremony. When he realized the Union regiments were shifting from "order arms" to the "carry" (the soldiers' salute of honor) he wheeled on his horse, dipped his sword and ordered the Confederate infantry to do likewise. Honor answered honor in ghostly silence with no trumpets, nor drums. (US National Archives)

INDEX

(References to illustrations are shown in **bold**. Plates are shown with caption locators in brackets.)